WILD MUSTANGS

PARLEY J. PASKETT

UTAH STATE
UNIVERSITY
PRESS
LOGAN, UTAH
84322-9515

Grateful acknowledgment is made to Little, Brown and Company for permission to use poetry from The Mustangs *by J. Frank Dobie, copyright 1934, 1951, 1952 by The Curtis Publishing Company; copyright 1936, 1949, 1950, 1951, 1952 by J. Frank Dobie.*

Library of Congress Cataloging-in-Publication Data

Paskett, Parley J., 1918–
  Wild mustangs.

  (The Western Experience)
  1. Wild horses—West (U.S.)—Anecdotes.   2. Mustang.
3. Horses—West (U.S.)—Anecdotes.   4. Horses—West
(U.S.)—Training.   5. Paskett, Parley J., 1918–
I. Title.   II. Series.
SF360.3.U6P37 1986   636.1'3   86–13165
ISBN 0-87421-126-3 (pbk.)

Table of Contents

Acknowledgment

I give thanks and appreciation to Professor Charles S. Peterson for taking the time from his busy, demanding schedule to write the introduction for *Wild Mustangs*. His historical narrative, drawn from great personal knowledge and much research, leads gently into the time and conditions surrounding these happenings.

Parley J. Paskett, Metropolis, Nevada, 1964.

I, Parley Johnson Paskett, was born in Grouse Creek, Box Elder County, Utah, May 21, 1918, to Sidney and Alice Johnson Paskett.

At the age of two I was given a calico pinto mustang filly and from then my attention and desires were drawn toward horses. Being reared on a farm, I've had a taste of all the experiences associated with farm life: how to feed and care for various animals, how to milk a cow, gather the eggs, slop the hogs—even how to dress out these animals for table use. I started riding horses at an early age and the spring I became nine years old I was privileged to go with my father on the spring horse roundup. I mostly rode an old bench-legged horse named "Star" that first year, but at age ten I broke a two-year-old filly Dad had given me. My experience grew rapidly from there.

Foreword

A mustang is a wild horse, a broomtail, a cayuse, a fantail, or any of several other terms cowboys use to describe this tame animal gone wild. To you, my children, and your children and theirs, I give this book of stories about mustangs. The action and excitement I experienced while capturing mustangs are described here.

Using helicopters today to run down wild horses removes both the thrill and sport in their capture. It was surely more exciting and certainly a greater challenge to pit a saddle horse and rider against the fear and speed of a wild horse. The better conditioning of the saddle horse and the knowledge the man had of his quarry were the main advantages the cowboy had over his wild friend, the mustang.

I call the mustang a friend to the cowboy because hundreds of these animals were captured and, after breaking, became fine saddle horses. When I rode for the Utah Construction Company, we had nearly two hundred saddle horses in the cavy during the summer work season until the cattle were on winter feed grounds or desert range. Over half of these horses were captured mustangs.

Nearly sixty mustangs—potential saddle horses—were captured each year, animals ranging from four to seven years old with few exceptions. A mustang stud was not considered too old to break to ride until he was past seven, and then only because his useful life span was shortened by age. The prime of life for a working saddle horse ranges from about seven to twelve years.

I hope you can feel some of the thrills I experienced with the mustangs as you read the following stories.

Parley J Paskett

Introduction

By Charles S. Peterson

Parley Paskett was one of the last generation involved in the West's great wild horse hunt. In this book, he recounts his own experiences in that adventure. His narratives are the product of a romantic age. Paskett himself is a romantic and draws upon the spirit of writers like Owen Wister, Zane Grey, and Frank Dobie. In more important ways, however, his stories reflect the deep traditions from which these writers drew.

Paskett is a storyteller of the first order. Experience is at the heart of his narrative. He is matter-of-fact and pragmatic not only about his stories but also about horses themselves and about the demands of life that led to the use of horses. This no-nonsense disposition extends to the entire range of horse-related emotion and conduct, including cruelty and tragedy as well as adventure, pride, and satisfaction. Paskett participated in the last two decades of an episode in history that lasted 400 years. Horses still ran free in Nevada by the tens of thousands.

To see Paskett's experience in context readers should consider the wild horse itself, northern Nevada's cold desert setting, and the ranching and family background from which he came. The wild horse story began early in America. Indeed the horse was indigenous to the western hemisphere. Evolving from geological eras, it migrated to Asia via the Bering Straits and spread to Europe and Africa. In America, however, horses became extinct about 10,000 years ago. In the "old world," they were domesticated by 2500 B.C. and adapted to military, economic, and other human needs. At least three types of horses emerged, two small and one large. From the small came the ancestors of the Arabian and Barb breeds of North Africa and the Iberian Peninsula. From the large came the tall, "feather legged" forest horse of northern Europe, ancestor to the great war horses of medieval times and the draft breeds of the late nineteenth century.[1]

In a "return of the native," horses were reintroduced to America by the Spanish after 1540. From Mexico, they spread northward into the

American West and after 1650 were acquired by Indians through trade and theft. Other horses migrated West from the eastern seaboard. Inevitably many were lost and became the foundation stock of free-roaming herds made up of what should properly be termed feral horses, because they were domesticated animals returned to a wild state. By the time of the Lewis and Clark expedition (1803–1806) and the exploration of Zebulon Pike (1805–1806), they existed in large numbers throughout the Great Plains and the Rocky Mountains. In the decades that followed, as one enthusiastic writer of the 1930s put it, horses "captured the West," in one of the world's most "momentous" developments. It was, he thought, "the greatest animal epic ever enacted."[2]

The post-Civil War era was the heyday of wild horses. They ranged throughout the West in large numbers. They were both resource and nuisance to advancing whites, and they transformed life for many Indian tribes. On the Plains their numbers first surged, as the buffalo were exterminated, and then receded as livestock and homestead frontiers advanced. Horses had been killed for their hides or to keep numbers in check as early as Spanish times. Now a generation-long chase ensued as cowboying Americans gradually forced wild horses into more remote localities. The weakest succumbed or were captured. Survivors were the wildest and the strongest. Crossed with well-bred "escapees," their progeny were good keepers, tough and fast. They were brilliantly colored and, when in good flesh, strikingly beautiful in their wilderness surroundings. Stallions of particular beauty and speed managed their bands with courage and intelligence, fostering legends of "white" or "pacing" or "fighting" studs in almost every locality.[3]

Some of the best were captured and used for cow ponies, making economic contributions that were unreckoned but particularly important to smaller stockmen struggling to get a start. Footloose cowboys "mustanged" to acquire a trading stock, or to take advantage of bounties and hide markets. Most ranchers, however, preferred better horses and by the 1880s were importing well-bred stallions. By the end of the century, some ranchers crossed Standardbred and Percheron stallions with wild mares and regularly harvested the get to sell as saddle or light harness horses and "farm or freight chunks." Under these circumstances, the largest wild horse populations had retreated by 1900 to the desert regions of the mountain West, where hunting and capture continued.[4]

Drought, bad winters, panics, and wars all influenced mustanging. During the panics of 1873 and 1894, wild horses were not worth catching. Drought made it apparent that they ate forage required by cattle, thus leading to increased efforts to reduce their numbers.[5] War created good markets. Yet ironically the United States Army never looked on wild horses favorably and rarely used them in the Civil and Indian wars. However, during the Spanish-American War and particularly England's Boer War and World War I hundreds of thousands of American horses were exported. Among the most famous wild horse depots was Miles City, Montana. There Paul Young, an itinerant Utah bronc stomper who won his spurs on Nevada mustangs, topped out about fifty broncos each day, demonstrating to army buyers from France and England during World War I that the "rough broke" broncos could be ridden. In all he rode about 4,000 wild horses during a period of four months. With "eight to ten bronc riders" employed, upwards of 32,000 horses "were brought in and sold for $145 to $185 per head."[6] Driven by high prices, horse exports surged to 51,150 in 1898, 103,000 in 1903, and to an all-time high of 357,553 in 1916 when France and England bought heavily.[7]

In spite of exports and aggressive hunting, wild horses were still numerous in the desert and Rocky Mountain states in the early twentieth century. Some guessed a million head were still to be found in 1925. Others reported a half-million were at large in 1930, but more reliable reports estimated "between 50,000 and 150,000" ran on the public domain, suggesting the total figure was far smaller. Exclusive of Nevada, where numbers were largest, the wild horse population in western states approximated only 25,000 in 1939, according to another estimate.[8]

Literary interest in wild horses was at its zenith in the decades after 1900. Zane Grey introduced millions to wild horse fantasies in southern Utah and northern Arizona. More serious writers in Texas extolled the wild horse and inflated the tradition. Journalists by the score wrote avidly of the adventure involved. Nostalgia was strong as people sensed the impending end of an era, and aging cowboys recalled past exploits.[9]

It was also an era of dramatic change as new infusions of blood and breed altered wild horse lines. Stockmen like the Sharps of Utah's West Desert introduced pedigreed work stallions. Elsewhere, increasing numbers of "escapees" joined wild herds. An even greater genetic infusion came after 1925 when work horses replaced by tractors were abandoned on the public domain. "Oregon Lummoxes" (Clydesdale crosses) and "Percheron Puddin'-Foots" now lent sinew and bone to feral herds, and Standardbred, Morgan, and Thoroughbred crosses made for lines of lesser size but greater dexterity, beauty, and speed. Nevertheless, remnants of short-coupled, fine-headed Spanish lines still existed.[10]

During this time all-out war was waged against wild horses. Determined professional hunters took to the field, and livestock men killed off the last herds. Chicken and pet food plants flourished and recreational killing was pursued with new enthusiasm. In northern Arizona, whites hunted wild horses relentlessly, forcing them into Navajo country in such numbers that a quarter of a million Indian ponies devastated ranges. This was followed by reduction programs that are still remembered bitterly by Navajos. On Utah's West Desert, David Sharp systematically shot "native stallions" to allow his pedigreed studs to breed broomtail mares. Using "a big old .44 pistol with a barrel about" a foot-and-a-half long, he "shot hundreds of them." In Utah's canyonlands, cattlemen Jim and Albert Scorup "spent whole days shooting" broomtail horses, sometimes killing "700 at a time." Natural Bridges promoter Zeke Johnson reported he helped exterminate San Juan County's last thousand head, 250 of which were crowded over a slickrock cliff, plunging to their deaths in a sickening practice that likely gave name to the famed Dead Horse Point overlook of the Colorado River. In Wyoming and Montana, desperate livestock counties conducted annual roundups. In the Big Horn Basin alone, 22,000 horses were shipped by one buyer in 1933 and 1934. Oregon's deserts also had famous horse hunters, one of whom conducted chases with airplanes and gathered 10,000 horses during the 1930s.[11]

But in few states did the drama and tragedy reach higher pitch than in Nevada. The intermittent playas and mountains of its vast deserts provided an ideal refuge, and 100,000 horses were reported in 1910. Stockmen controlled the legislature, and bounty laws were first passed and then revoked as bounty shooters killed branded animals as well as wild. Forest reserves were promoted as a means of control, and the Forest Service was authorized to eradicate horses. In 1908 plans were made to kill 15,000 on the reserves of Lander County alone, and mustanger Pete Barnum attracted brief national fame with a "revolutionary" canvas trapping corral. In the 1920s the Nevada legislature reversed itself, limiting the numbers of horses that could be removed, but stockmen "harvested" enough to keep some damper on growth. By 1940 large numbers of wild horses were still found on northern Nevada's ranges. In Elko County, where Parley Paskett spent most of his time, the Grazing Service reported that "only a small percentage" had been "removed."[12]

More important for the wild horses' future, however, was the Taylor Grazing Act of 1934. Bringing the public domain under regulation, it placed most of the wild horses in the West under the auspices of the Grazing Service, later the Bureau of Land Management, and set the stage for the development of a national wild horse policy. After decades of romantic interest and uncoordinated efforts to deal with feral horses, they became part of the conservationist crusade in the post-World War II period. Pushed by Nevada's Velma Johnson ("Wild Horse Annie"), laws were passed in 1959 and 1971 protecting horses on the public domain and regulating their disposition. Reserves were created in Nevada and along the Montana-Wyoming border, and small wild horse bands persisted on the public lands elsewhere. In 1971 wild horses on BLM lands numbered no more than 17,000, but by 1978 they had rebounded to 50,000 head, about 23,000 of which were in Nevada, with Wyoming following with nearly 9,000 horses. At that time, major efforts were made to dispose of surplus wild horses and burros through "adopt a horse" programs, and nearly 10,000 were placed with adopters at a cost of approximately $450 per animal.[13]

In recent decades the national mood has spawned a more scientific if less intimate and dependent interest in wild horses. New champions study them in their feral relationships, photograph them, and present them in writing and video film. Management practices are now based on recorded empirical information about characteristics and habits previously known, if at all, to only a handful of wild horse runners. In addition, new champions bring a long-distance intensity to our thoughts and feelings about wild horses. The new mood is earnest and optimistic but, for all its scientific pretensions, quite as romantic as any earlier frame of mind. There is no question that the remaining feral herds benefit. In the immediate sense, the modern mindset is more humane if less pragmatic than the moods that moved Parley Paskett and his predecessors. It has a luxury in its spatial and economic distances unknown to stockmen for whom competing wild horses could spell defeat. These distances also make us spectators in the wild horse drama rather than actors, although the growing awareness of an environ-mental ethic recognizes that humans and all other species may be par-ticipants in a catastrophic countdown as the limits of global support are approached.[14]

Nowhere have twentieth century Americans worked more directly with wild horses than in the cold deserts of northern Nevada and surrounding areas. There the environment both attracted wild horses and kept the human population low. It is a vast and isolated region lying primarily in the Great Basin but extending into the Snake River drainage. The country consists of flat alkali playas and rough desert floors intersected by localized mountain ranges. The latter run primarily north and south, many rising to 8,000 feet elevation. From them, streams flow into three general drainages: the Humboldt River, which runs southwestwardly to ultimately lose itself in the desert; the Snake River of the Columbia drainage; and the Great Salt Lake. Few in number, these streams are literally the blood of life to the cold deserts.[15]

Robbed of ocean moisture by the Sierra Nevada and Cascade ranges, the cold deserts are among America's most arid and fragile environ-ments. Precipitation falls mainly in the winter when it is too cold for plants to grow. Nevertheless, in its pristine condition the cold desert had achieved a simple but stable equilibrium in which sage-brush/grasslands plant communities covered thousands of square miles. Several species of sagebrush were found but had little feed value for cattle. By contrast bunchgrass and the herbaceous portion of the pristine plant communities were valuable for cattle and horses, but highly vulnerable when heavy or improperly timed grazing interfered with seed development and reseeding. In a few years, virgin stands were depleted, the equilibrium disrupted, and ranges opened for less useful plants.[16]

The first settlers were squatters who took out small ranches along the streams. These were soon supplanted by larger outfits from Cali-fornia and Texas, and ranches with Spanish names like the Rancho Grande and San Jacinto appeared. Others, like the Winecup and the Shoesole, took their names from early brands. To take advantage of somewhat more moderate weather, some ranchers wintered on flats and playas south and west of Wendover in what was locally called "the Great American Desert." Some extended onto the lush meadows of the Snake River in the neighborhood of what became Twin Falls, Idaho.[17]

The most prominent of the wayfaring Californians and Texans were respectively Jasper Harrell and John Sparks. The two ultimately joined forces as Sparks-Harrell and acquired many of the ranches in Elko County and adjacent Idaho. Using the "rubber forty" technique, they stretched patented control of streams and water holes to hundreds of thousands of acres of the public domain. In addition they took advantage of Nevada's extremely favorable state lands law to patent vast tracts of alpine pastures, which they fenced and utilized to control surrounding areas.[18]

Sparks and Harrell were high-handed at times. They were particularly aggressive in establishing "deadlines" beyond which sheep were not allowed and in importing gunmen to enforce these deadlines. None was more notorious than Diamondfield Jack Davis. A noisy braggart, Davis talked often and loudly of killing sheepmen and was indicted for the murder of two Mormon herders in 1896. Davis's defense was funded by cattlemen, primarily Sparks and Harrell. Two other Sparks-Harrell employees ultimately confessed, saving Diamondfield Jack's life without convincingly proving his innocence.[19]

By 1882 Sparks-Harrell had upwards of 75,000 cattle on their Elko County-Snake River ranges. Little winter feeding was practiced and much of their land was badly overgrazed. Yet all went reasonably well until the "white winter" of 1890. Little grass existed and what there was could not be reached. Cattle either ate nothing or ate sagebrush, which provided few nutrients and failed to generate heat in the digestive system to fend off cold. By spring 35,000 cattle were dead. According to some reports, a person could "walk on dead cows" for a hundred miles along the Mary's River, an affluent of the Humboldt. Many ranchers did not survive. Indeed, John Tinnin, Sparks's earlier partner, was ruined. Sparks and Harrell, however, pulled through, although neither had the same interest in the country as before.[20]

In 1908 the Sparks-Harrell outfit was sold to a Utah consortium called the Vineyard Company. Two years later the Utah Construction Company took the operation over and by 1920 ran about three million acres of land. Of this they owned 600,000 acres, leased 400,000, and controlled two million acres of public domain. In all the UC had some sixty ranches in Nevada and neighboring parts of Idaho and Utah. Although its numbers were down from the Sparks-Harrell heyday, it ran 52,000 cattle. After 1913 it also had 42,000 sheep, which grazed around the perimeters of its public domain range as a less violent but more effective substitute for the sheep deadline of the Sparks-Harrell era. The UC also ran some 3,000 head of horses to raise draft animals for their construction projects and replacement horses for ranching operations.[21]

The Utah Construction Company employed 250 men on its ranches. A longtime employee was Sidney Paskett, father of Parley, who also jobbed for the company and other livestock men in the region.[22] Sidney, who worked for the UC for decades, knew its operations as few men. He, more than Parley, gives continuity and the perspective of passing decades to the Paskett wild horse narratives, although each of the experiences described by Parley in this book is his own.[23]

Parley Paskett's grandparents first moved to Grouse Creek, near the northwestern border of Utah, in 1876. In the beginning they were farmers. Soon, however, they learned they were dependent upon grazing in their desert country. The Pasketts and their relatives ran a few cattle. Some of their Grouse Creek neighbors ran more than a few. Horses were central to the lives of all of them.[24]

This was more true for Sidney Paskett than most. Tall, ramrod straight, and agile, he was a man of endurance, patience, and good judgment. Throughout his days his dream was to own an independent outfit. He came close at times but worked for others, mostly the UC, except in the final years of his life when, in a last ditch effort to fulfill his life-long dream, he leased ranches for a few years. As late as 1953 he was still working at $150 a month plus a house and the privilege to range a few animals on the owner's ranch. In many respects he epitomized the literary ideal of a man made good by his contact with nature. He was wise and successful in his relationships with men and practical, yet humane, in his management of animals. He worked in harmony with animals, liking and managing them with skill and satisfaction. He was responsive to the environment, understanding the possibilities and limitations of the cold desert ranges. As wagon boss, hay contractor, and ranch foreman he worked for the UC from 1910 to 1953 with some breaks.[25]

In the middle of all this he owned horses himself. To launch the enterprise he bought approximately 100 head in 1922. They were mostly work mares that he ran on the public domain, where they mixed with wild stock. He was struck hard by the first winter, which was of rare severity. Fully half his horses died, including the biggest and best mares.

Without money to buy the fine stallions he needed, he bred many of his mares artificially. Unfortunately, Sidney Paskett's start in the draft horse business coincided with the move to farm tractors and a period of poor markets. Finding little sale for horses, he took haying contracts on the company's ranches at San Jacinto, Rancho Grande, and other hay ranches, putting his own horses to work. At its maximum, his herd numbered 250 head and ran on the open ranges, interbreeding with stock belonging to the UC and other outfits as well as unbranded broomtails.[26]

From age twelve Parley worked on the haying contracts and rode with his father in the annual horse roundups. He helped build traps at water holes and knew well the strategy of the chase. Before his mid-teens he had begun to accumulate the lore from which the accounts presented here were drawn. He knew the impact of cold winters and with his father faced up to the bitter pill of selling off the Paskett horses for "chicken feed." He saw horses run to death and otherwise abused, and he himself had the cowboy's pride in breaking wild horses others could not.

Parley also saw the loosely managed process of "natural" selection that was an accepted part of horse ranching in the Elko County area. In spite of efforts to capture the best horses, some of the "fittest" survived in the wild. Unless they ran directly with branded animals, they were technically unowned but were in effect a common resource for the ranching outfits on whose customary ranges they ran. Interbreeding with branded horses that used the same ranges, they became a secondary brood stock to which some management was extended. Purebred stallions and mares selected from the ranges were the UC's primary brood stock. These were held in fenced pastures during breeding season, after which the mares were turned onto the ranges, where they mixed with wild herds. Inevitably there were slip-ups. Mares that had not settled were bred by unbranded stallions. Other mares avoided the annual roundup and went wild for a colt or two. Wild horses as well as ranch-bred animals were gathered and the best selected for breaking. Others were shipped, or when prices did not justify the trouble of handling, turned loose again. During wild horse drives, as many as eighty young stallions were castrated and branded in a day's work and turned loose to mature. This practice was part of the process of raising replacement horses for work and riding purposes, but served also as a control on wild horse reproduction. There is no evidence that wild horses were killed wholesale on the UC ranges as they were else-where. They were often regarded as nuisances and their impact on the range was recognized, but they were an accepted if loosely managed part of the livestock operation.[27]

The wild horse of Parley Paskett's experience thus appears to have been a marginal animal. Poised between domestic use and the feral state in a ranching context that was itself in transition from last frontier to managed public lands and modern ranching, the wild horse was both symbol and resource. Thus poised, the wild horses of Paskett's stories are real, captured in his telling for a generation for whom symbol and resource have become one.

Notes

1. Historical treatment of the wild horse in America may be found in Francis Haines, *Horses in America: The Story of American Horses and their Riders from Eohippus of Prehistory to the Rodeos of Today* (New York: Thomas Y. Crowell Company, 1971); Walker D. Wyman, *The Wild Horse of the West* (Caldwell, Idaho: Caxton Printers, Ltd., 1963); and R.W. Howard, *The Horse in America* (New York: Follett Publishing Co., 1965). Each of these traces the early emergence of the horse, including its domestication and return to America. On the evolution of the draft horse from the medieval war horse, Howard's *The Horse in America*, pp. 168–80, is particularly good. A serious study of the burro is Frank Brookshier's *The Burro* (Norman: University of Oklahoma Press, 1974.) Less scholarly and more in the storytelling tradition of the West are books like J. Frank Dobie, *The Mustangs* (Boston: Little, Brown & Co., 1952); and Dobie, M.C. Boatright, and H.H. Ransom, *Mustangs and Cow Horses* (Austin: Texas Folklore Society, 1940). In addition, reminiscences featuring wild horses abound.

2. Howard, *The Horse in America*, pp. 19–30. The role of the Spanish in re-introducing the horse to the West is treated extensively in each of the books mentioned above and elsewhere. Among the best references are R.M Denhardt, "Spanish Horses and the New World," *The Historian* 1 (Winter 1938): 5–23; Denhardt, "The Southwestern Cow-Horse," *The Cattleman* (December 1938, January, February, March, April 1939): 21–23, 37–42, 39–45, 93–99, 34–36; Denhardt, "The Role of the Horse in the Social History of Early California," *Agricultural History* 14 (January 1940): 13–22; Wyman, *The Wild Horse of the West*, p. 67; and H.R. Sass, "Hoofs on the Prairie," *Country Gentleman* (July 1936): 5.

3. Legendary stallions show up often in the scholarly literature and, of course, in such sources as Zane Grey, in whose legendary stallions Frank Dobie discerned remarkable similarity to Texas "pacing white stallion" or "steed of the

plains" stories from the 1840s. Such legendry was still very much alive during the depression in northern Arizona, where I heard stories from older teenage boys of a pacing white stallion in the "Sinks" country northwest of Snowflake. These stories may well have been provoked by reading Grey, but they evoked vivid images in my mind and I know I would have vouched for their truthfulness.

4. Wyman, *The Wild Horse of the West*, pp. 132–45; David Sharp, Jr., Oral History Interview (May 18, 1974), Utah State University Library, pp. 1–5; Will C. Barnes, "Wild Horses," *McClures Magazine* 32 (January 1909): 185–94; Barnes, "The Passing of the Wild Horse," *American Forests* 30 (November 1924): 643–48; Barnes, "Wild Horses," *Atlantic Monthly* 134 (1924): 616–23; and Barnes "Wild Burros," *American Forests and Forest Life* 36 (October 1930): 640–42.

5. Haines, *Horses in America*, pp. 93–116; and Wyman, *The Wild Horse of the West*, pp. 113–26.

6. P.E. Young, *Back Trail of an Old Cowboy* (Lincoln: University of Nebraska Press, 1983), pp. 160–64 and 194.

7. Wyman, *The Wild Horse of the West*, pp. 120–23.

8. Ibid., pp. 149, 161, and 170–76; and Bruce E. Godfrey, "The Wild Horse Laws," *Utah Science* 40 (June 1979): 45–50.

9. Grey's wild horse novels are numerous. Among them are *Wild Horse Mesa* (1924); *Wildfire* (1917); and *The Last of the Plainsmen* (1908). Grey also eulogized wild horses frequently in articles, including "The Man Who Influenced Me Most," *American Magazine* (August 1926), where he credited Jim Emett of Lee's Ferry with teaching him to love horses. In words that both suggest the grassroots source of his story and help perpetuate similar legends, Grey wrote:

> I first saw Silvermane, the famous white-maned stallion, wildest of wild horses, when I was with Emett. I saw many others, and once Emett thought surely he had got me a glimpse of Wildfire. How the old gray-headed westerner would stand and gaze! To be sure, he wanted to capture those incomparable wild stallions, but I believed it was because he loved them. Whatever it was, I absorbed it in addition to my own thrilling emotion (p. 136).

Others who journalized on wild horses during the early decades of the century included Will Barnes and Rufus Steele, whose stories focused on Nevada and Utah.

10. From their operation at Vernon, Utah, the Sharps ran 1,500 upgraded broomtail mares that they bred to "thoroughbred . . . and Cleveland Bay . . . stallions." From this herd, they broke "about a hundred head of saddle horses every year." Sharp would then "take them out and peddle them." "The coach horse type" crosses weighed 1,200 to 1,300 pounds and "were always sold as farm chunks," David Sharp, Jr., Oral History Interview, Utah State University

Library pp. 1–2; and quoted from Dan Casement, "The Western Cowhorse," *The Producer* (March 1934): 3, by Wyman, *The Wild Horse of the West*, pp. 104 and 109.

11. Beginning in 1886, Navajo agents reported about 250,000 horses and ponies each year until 1891, when 118,789 were reported by a "careful census just completed by the Census Bureau." See reports of the Navajo agents in *Reports of the Commissioner of Indian Affairs*, 1886, p. 421; 1887, pp. 253–54; 1888, p. 190; 1889, p. 256; 1890, p. 161; and 1891, p. 309. Also see Richard White, *The Roots of Dependency: Subsistence, Environment, and Social Change among the Choctaws, Pawnees, and Navajos* (Lincoln: University of Nebraska Press, 1983), p. 220, which cites later estimates showing 100,000 head of Navajo horses in 1920 and estimates varying "from 40,000 to 80,000" in 1930. See also David Sharp, Jr., Oral History Interview, pp. 4–5; Neal Lambert, "Al Scorup, Cattleman of the Canyons," *Utah Historical Quarterly* 32 (Summer 1964): 307; and Wyman, *The Wild Horse of the West*, pp. 137, 157, and 158.

12. Wyman, *The Wild Horse of the West*, pp. 138–45 and 171; Barnes, "Wild Horses," *McClures Magazine* 32 (January 1909): 185–86; Rufus Steele, "Trapping Wild Horses in Nevada," *McClures Magazine* 34 (December 1909) 198–209; Steele, "Mustangs, Busters and Outlaws of the Nevada Wild Horse Country," *The American Magazine* (October 1911): 756–65.

13. Wyman, *The Wild Horse of the West*, pp. 165–76 provides a sketchy treatment of the Taylor Grazing Act's impact on Wild Horses; Mark Zarn, et al., *Wild, Free-Roaming Horses—An Annotated Bibliography*, USDA and USDI Technical Note 295 (Denver, 1977) provides an extensive bibliography for what may be termed the Wild and Free-Roaming Horse and Burro period. An excellent summary article is Godfrey, "The Wild Horse Laws," *Utah Science* 40 (June 1979): 44–50.

14. Godfrey, "The Wild Horse Laws," enquires if developments of recent years have solved problems as much as they have created them; Zarn, et al., *Wild, Free-Roaming Horses—An Annotated Bibliography* cites a good selection of publications to 1977; typical publications of the period are Hope Ryden, *Mustangs: A Return to the Wild* (New York: The Viking Press, 1972); and Skylar Hansen, *Roaming Free: Wild Horses of the American West* (Flagstaff: Northland Press, 1983), both of which are profusely illustrated with color photographs. A more scientific study is Kurt J. Nelson, *Sterilization of Dominant Males Will Not Limit Feral Horse Populations*, Research Paper RM-226, Rocky Mountain Forest and Range Experiment Station, USFS (December 1980). Humanistic rather than scientific or popular, but still part of the "Wild, Free-Roaming" era's reform mood is H.W. Marshall and R.E. Ahlborn, *Buckaroos in Paradise: Cowboy Life in Northern Nevada* (Lincoln: University of Nebraska Press, 1981); and Basil K. Crane, *Dust From an Alkali Flat: a Forest Ranger Remembers Central Nevada* (Reno: University of Nevada Press, 1984) reflects the era's political consciousness and humanitarian overtones in the way it treats wild horse stories.

15. The best treatment of Nevada's cold deserts as grazing country is in James A. Young and B. Abbott Sparks, *Cattle in the Cold Desert* (Logan: Utah State University Press, 1986), pp. 19–70. Less direct information about the cold desert environment may be found in Mike Hanley, with Ellis Lucia, *Owyhee Trails: The West's Forgotten Corner* (Caldwell: Caxton Printers, Ltd., 1973); Crane, *Dust From an Alkali Flat*; and Dale L. Morgan, *The Humboldt: Highroad of the West* (New York: Farrar & Rinehart, 1943.)

16. Young and Sparks, *Cattle in the Cold Desert*, pp. 24–35 and 63.

17. Ibid., pp. 37–55, 71–83, 89–99, and 101–115.

18. Ibid.

19. Ibid., pp. 220–23; and David H. Grover, *Diamondfield Jack: A Study in Frontier Justice* (Reno: University of Nevada Press, 1968).

20. John Sparks once said, "It is an unwritten law that a cattleman never talks of the size of his herd," but the *Elko Independent* reported that the earlier Sparks-Tinnin outfit ran 70,000 by 1883. See Young and Sparks, *Cattle in the Cold Desert*, pp. 102–3, also 121–36, and 199–214. Archie Bowman, who ran the same operation under the Utah Construction Company, was quoted as pegging the Sparks-Tinnin numbers at 175,000 in 1882, Nora L. Bowman, *Only the Mountains Remain* (Caldwell, Caxton Printers, Ltd., 1958), pp. 56–57.

21. Sterling Session, "Ogden's Wattis Brothers and the Utah Construction Company's Nevada Ranch," a paper read in Ogden, Utah, November 1978, makes reference to the horse operation of the Utah Construction Company. Also Bowman, *Only the Mountains Remain*, pp. 58–59, 192–93; and Parley Paskett telephone conversation with Charles Peterson, October 26, 1985. In its use of Percheron stallions, the UC followed national and regional preferences: Percheron stallion registrations outnumbered combined Shire and Clydesdale listings 70,000 to 20,000 in the 1920 Census, and by 102 to 33 in the 1909 Utah registry of purebred stallions. Francis Haines, *Horses in America*, pp. 170–71; and John T. Caine III, and H.J. Frederick, *Improvement of Utah Horses*, Bulletin No. 107, Utah Agricultural College Experiment Station (Logan: 1909), pp. 132–39.

22. Parley J. Paskett, *'Round the Campfire* (Provo: privately published, 1972). This family history focuses most squarely on the role of Sidney Paskett but shows the activities of his son Parley and other family members.

23. Ibid.

24. Ibid.

25. Ibid.

26. Ibid.; and Parley Paskett conversation with Charles Peterson, October 26, 1985.

27. Ibid.

The Mustang

The western mustang is a wild, hardy species of horse, if indeed it can be called a species. According to the *World Book Encyclopedia*, colonists found no horses when they came to North America. American Indians did not know of them until Spanish conquerors under Hernando Cortez came to Mexico in 1519. Cortez and later explorers may have left horses behind and they probably became the ancestors of the wild horses of the western plains.

At first the Indians feared the horses, making it easier for the Spaniards to conquer them. Not until around 1600 did Indians start using horses.

Many of the fine war horses Cortez brought to Mexico were of Arabian origin. Gelding the male horse was not a common practice. Thus when horses were freed in battle or through other circumstances, they began to multiply. Some descendants of those horses still have many fine Arabian characteristics, while others have long, ugly heads and ill-shaped bodies. The latter are probably descendants of draft horses crossed with the Arabian, then inbred, father to daughter, over several generations.

Toughness has remained with the mustang over the years. Slower, less intelligent, and less hardy animals fall prey to predators and inclement elements such as heavy snow and long droughts.

The hooves of mustangs are not harder than other horses reared on the range. The black hoof has a tougher shell than the white hoof, but either animal, mustang or domestic, will develop a softer shell if kept in a wet corral or damp meadow ground for long periods. I have found that a mustang, when ridden, needs shoes the same as the domestically raised horse, this because of the extra load he carries and the longer distance he travels as a saddle horse.

One year of a horse's life is equal to about three of a man's. So a seven-year-old horse is equal in age to a twenty-one-year-old man. This coincides with the experience I had with saddle horses. The prime life span is from about ages seven to twelve, varying with the use and care given the horse. Excellent care during his early years could develop his size, strength, and stamina much faster, extending the prime years of life to about ages five to twelve. Horses can be worked and ridden much younger than five, but care should be given to not overdo the animal, killing its spirit or desire and thus its use.

Mustangs in separate regions of the West have different characteristics. The mustangs I encountered on Nine Mile Mountain were of good quality. Several were grays and roans and had well-proportioned bodies, small, refined heads, and were very intelligent. Most of them were capable of being good saddle horses. Not so with the mustangs on the Steptoe Valley desert. Along with many beautiful animals there were some with long, ugly heads, swaybacks, crooked legs, and coarse, protruding hip bones. Probably half of them would never weigh over eight hundred pounds.

Horses are very intelligent and can be taught many things. A good cow horse can spot the animal you want to cut from the herd almost as quickly as you see it. The properly trained rope horse knows how to throw his weight against the rope to absorb the shock of the animal being stopped and knows where to run so you have the best opportunity to catch, at times resisting your guidance as bad judgment.

A horse gets sleepy the same as a man. If ridden through the day and into the night he may get drowsy and stumble or stagger. The horse sleeps on its feet, laying out flat only when really tired from travel or hard work. An old cowboy saying is that a horse is worth one hundred dollars for each time it can roll completely over after a day's ride. If that is true, many saddle horses would have to be classed as duds.

Mustangs on the Range

We were handling near two thousand branded range horses inter-mingled with about twelve hundred wild, unbranded mustangs. The horses ranged from the Great Salt Lake Desert on the east to the Idaho border on the north. They spilled over Highway 93 on the west, and to the south the border was near Whitehorse Pass along Highway 50 out of Wendover.

There were 250 horses belonging to my father, Sidney Paskett, his brother, George, and myself. There were also many horses, privately owned, that are not counted in this reckoning. The main body of the horses belonged to the Utah Construction Company and were branded with the Wine Cup iron.

We captured mustangs any way that we could, and when we caught them we claimed them as our own if we were working for ourselves. They went to the ranching company if we were hired out. Most of the horses were small; very few were as heavy as eleven hundred pounds. The average run of them was from six hundred to one thousand pounds. The small mares were useful only as kid ponies and broodmares.

When you capture the wild mustang it takes away that illusory—almost mythical—deceptive appearance that has surrounded the wild animal. He is no longer the untouchable that has eluded man for such a time. He is now merely a captured animal to be trained for man's use. Until thoroughbreds and quarter horses came into the western picture, mustangs were the main source of saddle horses. They were tough and hardy, very useful to the cowboy.

It was early in April and we had gathered the last of nearly four hundred range horses from Squaw Creek and areas near there. The horses were grazing east of the corral. In a few minutes we would corral them, cut out the young animals to be broken to ride or work, brand the "slicks," and castrate the studs.

I heard Dad call to me and saw he was waving for me to come to him. There seemed to be no urgency, so I slowly rode to him.

"Do you remember the two yearlings we saw mating last spring—that little buckskin filly with the white front stocking and the red roan stud?" he asked as I approached. He was motioning toward a small, rough-looking animal that was suckling a skinny runt of a colt.

"Yes, I do remember," I said.

"That looks like the filly to me. What do you think?"

"I don't remember ever seeing any other animal with such a high front stocking and the buckskin color. You must be right," I said.

Dad commented, "It was a real oddity to see two yearlings mate. I've never seen that before. To see a colt mothered by a two-year-old filly is hard to believe."

The evidence was there before our eyes, and though we didn't know the actual birthday of the filly we did conclude from what we remembered that she was bred at one year old, give or take a month or two. She conceived and had a foal or colt at age two. I have never seen this happen before or since and have questioned other stockmen who have never witnessed such an occurrence.

Mustangs run in bands, bunches, herds, whatever you want to call them, of up to fifteen head. An average bunch is seven to ten and is controlled by one stud. There may be one or two yearling studs in the band, but when they become two years old the monarch, or herd stud, whips them out. These young studs then band together, two to five in a bunch, and run as bachelors until they are able to steal a mare for themselves.

It is easy to see what happens to a band of mustangs when left alone to range and reproduce naturally. One day I was riding in an area about ten to twelve miles south of Shafter, Nevada, at a place called the Ryegrass Patch. It is a hardpan area dotted with humps of half-dead greasewood and saltbrush and is flooded each spring. The day I was there, the deepest water I got into was near to my horse's knees. He was not a pony horse and I guessed the water to be between fourteen and eighteen inches deep. It covered an area of maybe forty acres, maybe eighty. I don't have any idea.

That day horses were coming in from every direction to water. Most of them had been out two or three days and were gaunt and extremely thirsty. My horse was standing well out in the water, and these bands of mustangs converged around us like a bunch of chickens after grain was thrown to them. They came as near as twenty to twenty-five yards and kept the distance from me, but never did they scare enough to run away. I rode out through the water, admiring the beautiful animals and the array of colors. Many herds of six to nine head were exact carbon copies of each other.

There were eight palominos in one bunch and I thought I'd try for one of them, but seven black horses with wide bally faces, each with four white legs, stood off to my right and I thought, maybe one of them. Behind them, however, was a bunch of eight steel-gray horses with silver manes and tails, bally faces, and white legs. To one side of them was a bunch of ten light sorrels; they also had bally faces and white legs, and near them were eight red sorrels with no white on them whatever. A short distance from them were six head of blood bays and a bunch of browns and several mixed bunches, as though a determined stud may have stolen a mare from each of the different bands.

The older studs had coarse jaws, heavy necks, and long, tangled manes and tails, much longer manes than their counterparts raised in the mountainous country where the brush and trees combed them regularly as they ran. Younger studs were easily recognized, cagey in their actions. Some were in small groups of three to five and some had already picked up a mare or two, starting a band of their own. One particular young stud I noticed had two young mares his same color. I guessed the old monarch had whipped the young stud from the bunch but had more mares than he could control, so the younger stud took two of them with him.

We called breeding father to daughter and brother to sister or mother in-breeding, and believed it would bring out or emphasize the poorer qualities in the animal. Some horsemen, mainly thoroughbred breeders, bred father to daughter trying to strengthen the finer qualities of their horses. I expect it could work either way or maybe both ways on the same animal. This was called line-breeding.

Some of these mustangs were small and ill-shaped animals, while others were very refined and beautiful to behold. The black ballys were larger than most of the others, as were the steel-grays. I would have been happy with one of them.

Have you ever seen more than two hundred wild mustangs all running the same direction at the same time? Have you wondered what you might do with them when they got to the corral? Have you ever wished you could be twenty riders on twenty good thoroughbred saddle horses so you could keep all these bands of mustangs going the right direction, so you could tuck in the bunches along the edges instead of having to let them go?

In the ardor, the zeal, the passion, the ecstasy of the moment, I stood high in my stirrups and galloped those horses mile after mile, wanting so much to save a good band yet not being able to actually choose which bunch might continue in the right direction. I was able to keep nine of mixed color and not the best conformation; however, one was a "grulla" dun mare with a palomino colt and there were two young studs, both brown, that probably would grow to be good saddle horses.

That day was one of the most fun days I can remember. I suppose that is because of the enormity of the situation, the many horses, and the several colors and herd compositions of the wild mustangs. It still thrills me to remember that day and the race I had with so many mustangs. In my mind I can see them scattered over a large area, sometimes running in separate bunches. When they did mix, the studs would squeal and bite and kick, each protecting his own. Going up the valley, most of the bands were led by older mares, but when they turned back on me the monarch studs took the lead, and each was a magnificent picture as he guided his little harem back to the wilds. The stud ran ten to fifteen yards ahead of his band and they followed generally in single file.

One band of eight sorrels led by a large, brown stud came close to me and I tried to catch them, but they were too fast and too intent on remaining free. They were look-alikes except for the stud, and I believe the former monarch was sorrel and had gotten too old to defend his harem and so was whipped away by the younger, more virile brown stud.

As I watched many horses grow up around me I noticed that about half of the two-year-old fillies conceived, giving birth to colts at age three. About four out of ten of those missed foaling the following year at age four, but were quite regular from ages five to ten. A mare that became pregnant at age three or four gave birth to a colt each following spring with few exceptions. On rare occasions a mare stayed barren until ten to twelve and then gave birth to a colt each spring until fifteen or near that age. Some few mares remained barren. A mare on good feed and in strong physical condition can bring a foal each year until quite old. If her condition is not adequate she may bring a runt or deformed colt in her later years.

The reproduction of horses that run on the range both winter and summer without supplement, as mustangs do, depends largely on the feed available and the intensity or severity of the winters. Rough winters kill the old, the crippled, and the mares with foal, especially the young two year olds and the older, weaker mares. A rough, deep-snow winter, however, brings good grass in the spring and fattens the horses. They flourish and the mares become pregnant, bringing a bumper crop the following spring. Following these severe winters you find some yearlings come through the winter and the mother dies. This is because the yearling has suckled the mother, draining her strength. When the spring comes and the mud makes traveling heavy, the mare can't muster strength enough to change from the rough winter feed to the washy spring feed and dies after bringing the yearling through far enough so it survives.

It's a rough, cruel world, strictly survival of the fittest whether it be an ugly, ill-shaped mustang or one of refinement and beauty.

Mustang Roundup

The company runner crawled cautiously up to my foxhole near Kamberg, Germany, two days before we breached the Siegfried Line. He had some mail clutched tightly in his hand.

"Some letters for you, Sarge. Captain said to read them and be certain they're burned before we move out. You better hurry, Sarge. Sorry I couldn't get to you before but sometimes it's not safe up here with you guys."

I was Sergeant over a machine gun section in the 69th Infantry and it was dangerous where I worked. Larsen was a good kid, just past twenty years old and should have been home going to school. He had lots of courage and there were days when he needed all of it.

"Captain said to tell you we move out at 0815. We're to take those two high hills ahead of us. We've been getting sniper fire from the one on the right. Third platoon sent a couple men out to quiet the sniper." Larsen counted out my mail.

"You have seven letters, Sarge. That's a lot of mail. Must be someone wants you to come home."

"I hope so, Larsen," I said as I shuffled through the letters. Of course they were all important, but the one from my father is what caught my eye. It was only the second letter from him in the three years I had been in the army. I opened it first.

"Before you get too deeply engrossed, Sarge," Larsen said, "can you tell me what the static is on our right flank? I was supposed to find out for the Captain."

"Ya, Larsen. It's a machine gun nest behind the clump of brush near the end of the ridge. Keep your head down, now. Those boys are shooting at everything in sight. They're nervous. There's a pillbox behind the nest. Tell the Captain I'll take out the machine gun nest, and I think the pillbox people will give up when we pass them by. Anything more?"

"Nope. I'll be on my way, Sarge. Good luck to you." Larsen slithered off toward the command post. I got back to the letter. It was pages long. Dad was evidently making up for the many times he wanted to write but didn't.

Dear Son,

I hope you are all right. Your mother and I pray every day for your safe return, and that the war will soon be over. May God bless you, Son.

It is hard to get good help now that all of you young fellows are in the war and I have worked many long hours, from before daylight until after dark. I don't know how long I can keep this up.

One bright spot was when Johny Kincaid came back to work for me. You remember Johny. He is a real good rider and quite a mustanger. He's off the booze so I try and keep him out of town. I want to tell you of a couple instances that happened.

Johny and I were riding near the Delno mines on the north end of the mountain last fall, checking to see if there were any cattle where the guys at the mine might poach a little. We know they are honest but when a person gets hungry he could do something out of desperation he wouldn't do otherwise. Well, Johny rode down close to the shacks and I stayed out on the hill, just in case. I got to lookin' around and spotted a bunch of mustangs on the long ridge that meanders out toward Rock Spring Wash. It was a white stud and his bunch. I knew the horse and had tried to catch him several times. He was a pacer and quite a pretty horse. There were seven all told in the bunch.

I looked for Johny and could see he was coming back from the shacks at the mine. If he would hurry we might get a run at the horses who were grazing south over the brow of the big ridge.

Just before Johny came to me something familiar came into my view. You remember the old trap corral off the side of the big ridge? We went by there one day and you remember the net wire wing was still intact? In fact the corral was good enough to maybe hold a few head for a short time. Well, this white stud and his bunch were setting almost in the wings of that corral. If we hurried and started them before they grazed much further we might put them right into the corral and rope one before they could get away.

I waved at Johny to hurry the last few yards up to me and we got set for the race. I guess this is really why we rode up there in the first place.

Boy, that Johny is a good hand. We hit those mustangs perfectly and before they knew it we all piled up in the wings close to the corral gate. The stud hit the net wire head on and broke his neck, also a black mare did the same. One bay mare hit the net wire and slid under it. She got up unhurt and got away. I roped a sorrel two-year-old stud and Johny got a yearling stud, sort of gray in color. We couldn't have done better. I checked the mouth on the old white stud and he was smooth—probably twelve or more. Wish you could have been there.

This winter the snow has been awfully deep and is still heavy in many places, though we have had several warm days. It would have thrilled you to ride with Johny and me last month. We were trailing about thirty head of cattle from the Twenty-One Mile to the Eighteen when we saw four young studs on a snowy sidehill near Division Canyon.

I said, "Let's see if they can run in the deep snow, Johny. I'll ride out toward them and you take a cut on them. Maybe you can rope one."

"All right," says Johny and reached down and pulled on his latigo.

I rode out toward the studs and they didn't run. They couldn't run because they were too weak. I gathered them in like so many gentle cows and we trailed them to the ranch with the stock we had. I was sure they wouldn't know how to eat hay, and anyway a wad of it would kill them because their systems weren't working. I don't know what they had eaten, but surely not much. Tall sage and cedar trees were all that showed above the snow. We put them in the ryegrass field below the ranch.

We spent the next two days on the south end of Delno and gathered eighty-four head of mustangs. I didn't see the roan pacer or the gray $\overline{P}$ horse that I branded when he was two. He'd be twelve years old by now. Wish I had kept him to ride, but old Ted wanted him and I'd rather turn him loose than let Ted steal him from me. So I branded him and turned him loose.

We put all those mustangs in the field with the four and went to the H-D to try the wild horses on Knoll Mountain. We thought it would be worth a try while conditions were so much in our favor. We gathered twenty-three head. They were all we could find. I don't think many of the mustangs left out on the range around here will see the spring. Of course there are hundreds of them on the desert.

It's more fun to run them now we have some offspring from the Remount studs, broke to ride and in our cavy. Those half-thoroughbreds can sure run. A few of them can buck too. Crossed with some of those Percheron mares they get to weigh twelve to fourteen hundred, and that's a lot of horse to control if he wants to buck you off.

The Possum stud is a real good saddle horse. You broke him well and also Popeye and Abe. They are good horses. Long-legged Abe is quite a runner. Extra good on the range. He bucked old Jim Thomas off last fall, but it was Jim's fault. He cinched him too tight with his old center fire rig and failed to move Abe off center. Abe went straight in the air and in three jumps Jim was on the ground.

Well, hope to see you soon.

So Long,

Dad

I read the letter through three times, and only glanced at the other six, skimming them for news before setting them afire. Following this I crawled across the countryside until I was close enough to drop a rifle grenade into the machine gun nest. It was a perfect shot and we were back to the business of war, a business I would like to give away so I could go back to running mustangs, if there were any left to run.

The Love Trap

In the early 1930s cash money was not easy to come by. Anyone would trade, but the dollar was hard to obtain.

Fall came and my pockets were empty. Oh, I had worked all right, hard too, but breaking horses for oneself is not a moneymaking venture unless you can sell the horses, and there was no sale for them.

A friend of mine offered me a job herding a band of sheep through the winter and I accepted. He had eight hundred head that he ranged on the desert down in Steptoe Valley. "Take your rifle," he said, "you might see a coyote now and then and each prime pelt is worth five dollars." Five dollars isn't much, but six of them would be the same as a month's wages.

I rolled my extra clothes in my heavy, sheep-lined coat and draped the bundle across behind my saddle where I tied it with the saddle strings. My rifle boot was slung on the right side, rifle butt to the rear so I could draw it as I stepped off my horse if necessary. As an afterthought I pushed an old telescope into my pack, for no real reason at all. My hackamore fit nicely under the bridle of my horse, Suzy. Except for the nearly new seagrass rope that hung on the right of the saddle horn and the high-stepping Hambletonian mare, I was really decked out like a sheepherder.

We trailed to the desert and I was left with the sheep, a camp wagon, a team of mules, and my horse, Suzy. I had several sacks of oats but no hay. All the animals were expected to live off the land, the oats a supplement when feed was scarce. Suzy, of course, got her full share of oats and more.

My boss pointed out the approximate boundaries of the area where the sheep could graze, and he promised to visit me every six weeks. I watched the dust boil up behind his old Ford truck and realized that I was alone again, which was not so different. I had worked and lived alone most of the time.

While searching my new domain my keen eyes detected several

bands of horses at various distances and I knew that I was in wild horse country. My heart beat a little faster and I immediately started planning how I might catch one of those horses.

Six weeks passed and my boss returned to check on the sheep and bring me groceries as he had promised. He also brought two boxes of shells for my rifle. He told me the horses were mustangs and that several more bands would come to the desert floor as the snow deepened in the mountains.

"If you can catch one, he's yours," he said. "Just don't lose my sheep while you chase wild horses." I made a solemn promise not to desert the sheep for a mustang. The country was big and open and my boss knew it would be hard to lose a band of sheep.

The next few weeks I looked at many horses through that old telescope, grateful for the hunch that caused me to bring it along. Some bunches of mustangs run mostly to one color, generally following that of the monarch stallion. I noticed eight palominos in one bunch and eleven flax-maned sorrels in another. They were beautiful, and I grew anxious to get a closer look. But my presence unnerved them, and when they saw me riding near they would hurriedly move into a tight bunch, mill around, and gallop away, sometimes for several miles.

The snow came deep in the mountains and I could soon count over two hundred wild horses right from my camp by using the priceless old telescope. As winter progressed I rode near the horses continually and they became more accustomed to me. Their fear subsided and they no longer ran from my presence. They still bunched up and avoided me constantly, but I detected a weakening, an acceptance, and was hopeful that I might soon ride among them unchallenged.

Maybe I could pick out a nice stud and crease him with a rifle slug. I remembered my father telling me he had seen Indian Jack do it one time. "You have to be close enough to almost see the curl of the hair near the crest of the neck," he said. "If you shoot too high, you miss. If you shoot too low, you kill."

I knew there was just about two inches of cord along the crest of the neck to aim at. That isn't much, but I could clip the head off a sage-grouse at two hundred feet with my long-barreled 30-30, and I was certain I could hit that two-inch strip.

The next few days after having considered this, I rode the breaks and the draws up in the edge of the snow and killed seven coyotes for practice. Each one I hit close behind the ear and never missed a shot. I felt then that I was ready and I eagerly scanned the horses for the one I would try. Time after time I crept up on several horses only to be detected before I could get a shot away.

The last of January came and my boss returned. He was pleased with the condition of the sheep. I told him that I hadn't herded much and he said that was good, the sheep could feed better when left alone. Lazy herder—fat sheep. He was glad I had shot the coyotes before they got into the sheep, and he tossed the pelts into the back of the truck to sell for me. We moved the camp about five miles north while he was with me. When he suggested the move, I thought he might take me clear out of wild horse country but the five miles made no difference at all. There were horses all over the desert.

The third day after the move I saw a buckskin stud that looked good at a distance, and for the next few days I stalked him and his band of ten, studying each animal as well as I could through the telescope. There were seven mares, three that I judged to be yearlings, and the big boss. The stud was larger than most of the horses I had viewed. His conformation was good—a straight back, clean legs, a beautiful, arched neck, and an attractive head. His mane and tail were long, and even from the distance his lower jaw showed the coarseness of a full-aged stud. Maybe he was too old for me to break, yet something about him made me want to try. I was pleased with my discovery and made him the object of my pursuit, trailing him around day after day, never following when he would run, but always present in the daylight hours.

Early in March my patience and persistence started paying off and I rode near without exciting the band. This encouraged me considerably and I was sure my chance at the stud would soon come.

One day when the sun was bright and warm, I was sitting half asleep on a flat rock, part of a pile of boulders on the point of a low ridge about one-half mile above the valley floor. My rifle lay cradled across my legs and my filly, Suzy, was grazing less than twenty feet away. On the next ridge north was part of the buckskin stud's bunch. It was about a hundred yards to the closest one, and they were feeding contentedly, taking no notice of me.

I was wondering where the stud and the other four members of the band were when my Suzy nickered. She was answered almost immediately by a horse just below and back of me. Before I could move to see what was approaching, the beautiful buckskin stud walked into my view not more than fifty feet away. He tossed his head slightly and whinnied low. Suzy answered.

I could see his wide, black, fiery eyes and his long, black mane and tail. There were black tiger stripes near his knees and hocks and a dark strip running the full length of his back. His presence and beauty thrilled me clear through. Right then I named him Tiger because of his many black stripes.

I hesitated for only a moment, then carefully I raised my rifle and pulled the hammer back to full cock. The stud was looking at Suzy and had not yet seen me. He was in a perfect position with the sun shining on his arched neck. I located the curl in the hair at the crest and slowly brought my sights to bear on that tiny spot. I held my breath to be more steady yet my rifle wavered slightly. I let that breath out and took another. Gradually I brought the sight to bear on the target again. "Too high you miss, too low you kill." My eyes watered and I blinked to clear my vision. Now was the time—but I didn't shoot. The stud tossed his head and whinnied again, breaking my trance, and as Suzy answered him I knew I couldn't do it. My love for horses was too great to chance killing such a magnificent animal.

Slowly I lowered the rifle and let the hammer down to a half cock. I placed it again across my legs, never taking my eyes from the stud. Then he noticed my presence and emitted a loud whistle as he spun away, his great strides taking him through the rocks and brush in reckless abandon. I watched with fascination as he led his bunch on the wild run to the valley floor, going far out on the desert plain before circling back toward the ridges to the north.

My hands were shaking as I put my rifle back in the boot. Not only my hands but my whole frame quaked from excitement and anticipation. If the stud hadn't whinnied just when he did he could be lying dead there on the hillside. Why I ever considered shooting at him I shall never know.

Several days later I was in my camp wagon stoking a fire to cook lunch when I heard Suzy whinny and receive an answer from the stud. I looked out the door and could see the stud about a quarter mile away looking anxiously toward camp. His head was high and periodically he would whinny, and each time Suzy answered. She was pawing and dancing back and forth by the side of the camp. I had her tied to the wheel but it came to me that the rope might not hold her. With her prancing around it could come loose and she might be hard to catch. I pushed open the door and went out to check. It was tied solid. I stroked her neck and spoke quietly to her, but my talking and petting didn't calm her at all. She had eyes only for that wild stallion.

I soon discovered she was in heat, though it was a little early in the season, and that was the reason the stud was so interested.

My mind was in a whirl. How could I get the two of them together and be close enough to put a rope on him? I considered and discarded several ideas in rapid succession. If I could only sit under Suzy without her stepping on me and put a rope on the stud when he mounted to mate. I quickly thought of ways I might make that idea work. A hurried glance at the stud indicated that he was still interested and had approached to the far side of some serviceberry bushes.

That was it. I could walk alongside the mare and place her between two of those thick bushes, then tie that half-inch rope around the bottom of one bush and build a slipknot in the other end. When he mounted I would put the loop on his front leg and pull the slipknot tight.

Feverishly I worked to get the needed items for the trap. The rope was easy and the required knots took only a few minutes. I replaced the hackamore that was on Suzy with a bridle. Somehow I had to get the hackamore on the stud—but first I had to catch him.

My heart was pounding so hard I thought the stud might hear it and go away, but it wasn't so. He trotted around in little circles as I approached with the mare but gave no real indication he might leave and not return.

Soon the trap was set. Two serviceberry bushes with just the right distance between them were on the lower edge of the brush patch. Suzy was still excited and nickering when I led her into place. I hobbled her front feet to make sure she would stand still and not step on me, and when all was ready I squatted close under her left shoulder and against the serviceberry bush.

With me out of sight it took only a few minutes for the stud to come and investigate. I heard him walking toward us nickering anxiously. Suzy answered and tried to move but the hobble stopped her. There was a shuffling sound as the stud mounted and his left front foot came down by my shoulder. I nervously slid the rope up over the hoof and pulled it tight. I knew I had him foul but all is fair in love and war, and this was certainly love. Now if he didn't break a leg when he hit the rope every-thing would be just fine.

In a few seconds all hell broke loose. I came out from under the mare and the bush to keep her from stepping on me. The stud saw me right beside his head and fell back off the mare, whirling as he dismounted to get away. The mare crowded toward me, spooked at all the excitement. There was a crash and a grunt when the rope suddenly became tight on the stud's leg. He lunged to the left and the rope stopped him in midair on his second jump, flipping him hard to his side. When he landed his back was a little downhill and the rope was still very tight. The stud could struggle but couldn't get his feet to the ground to propel his body up.

Immediately I ran to put the hackamore on his head. Given the fear and fight in that buckskin stud, that was no easy task. I had him entangled and near helpless, so in spite of his screaming and kicking the hackamore was soon tied in place. I fastened the twenty-foot, half-inch lead rope to the bottom of a serviceberry bush and then cut the rope from the stud's leg. I smile as I remember how he fought long and hard. The rope held. The bush was solid. There wasn't the slightest chance he would get away.

Tiger became a good saddle horse, though hard to break because he was seven years old and wild as anything I ever saw. He filled out to weigh a thousand pounds when fat, and he had stamina and courage that was hard to equal.

The following spring Suzy had a buckskin colt that was a real beauty. I called him Tiger Two because of the dark stripes he inherited from his father.

The Chipmunk

"See the gray mare on the side of the mountain over there?" Gilbert was speaking to the new hand, Rusty Jones.

"Ya, I see her," Rusty replied.

"She's our bell mare," Gilbert added. "Do you think you could cross over the draw below her—meet her right in the pass and take her and the bunch north around the peak and back to camp? We'll wait here until you get started with 'em."

"Sure thing. You say she's the old bell mare?" Confidence welled up in Rusty's speech for he knew that bell mares were kept around with the cavy much of the time. He was new with the outfit and didn't know that the gray mare wearing the bell was the wildest, orneriest, most contemptible animal on the whole Squaw Creek Mountain. Three years ago was the last time she had seen the inside of a corral and it was then that she was given the bell. Several riders had gone after "the old gray bell mare" in those three years with no success at all. They came in shaking their heads only to be greeted by Gilbert with his almost-shy grin and then a chuckle.

"Where did you put the bell mare?" he would ask.

"She got away," would be the general answer.

"Got away? Can't you even be trusted to bring in an old gentle bell mare?" Then Gilbert would guffaw and the new hand receiving the butt of the joke would realize something was amiss. Today was no different and I could hear Gilbert chuckling as Rusty rode out of sight.

We watched Rusty cross the deep draw and climb toward the pass.

"It looks like he'll start them just right for us." Gilbert was more serious now. He was an ardent mustanger and had a premonition where each bunch would run in any given situation.

"Sid, they'll go around the peak to the north spring and come back on the heavy trails past the corner of the field over there." Gilbert pointed to the trails. "You pick them up there and take them down in the flat below Cobre to the old railroad tracks. They won't cross over the tracks so don't worry about that. Bring them to me at the point of the long cedar ridge next to the highway. I'll run them back to the top of Maverick Pass and they'll head for Independence Valley. Probably down that long ridge there." He pointed to a ridge just south of us and I could see the heavy trails on it even from the distance.

Gilbert then spoke to me. "Parley, you have the biggest job. When they hit those trails it will be almost impossible to turn them back. If they are about played out make a short circle and take them over toward Holburn Spring. We'll watch and see where they come back. If they are too strong, try to rope one of them. I would prefer the Chipmunk stud if possible. I sure want that stud. He's four this year and we need to get him soon if we want to break him to ride."

"All right, we'll try 'em." I said.

Sid was riding a brown that sported a prominent bump between his eyes and a long Roman nose. His ears were short and turned in at the top. Sid had ridden the horse four years before he felt entirely safe to dismount and mount when riding alone on the range. His run would be no great worry for such an aggressive mount. Gilbert's big white horse was especially good in the mountains so I had no misgivings there. My horse, Freckles, was strong and full of grain. He would be able to handle about anything that came my way, either in a race or on the rope.

We parted as soon as Rusty started the horses north, each going toward his assigned relay spot. I almost wished I had farther to ride because it was early spring and a chilling breeze blew in short gusts. I found a secluded spot under the brow of a hill sheltered from the wind by several cedars, yet open enough for me to observe the approach of the bell mare if everthing went right. I sat there hunched over in my saddle.

A clock watcher could never be a mustanger. Patience is most essential. A person might wait several hours and finally find that the horses have gone another direction, or he may not see them at all. There were several possibilities. Unless the bell mare and bunch crossed the highway today, which circumstance was very remote, they would probably come over the mountain somewhere in my vision. I fully expected they would follow the heavy trails out of Maverick Pass and come directly toward the place where I was waiting.

I divined that it would take about three hours for the bell mare and the bunch to travel the scenic tour. They were already on the north side of Squaw Creek Mountain, maybe as far around as North Spring. It would take another twenty or thirty minutes to climb from the spring to the high pass. If they came through this high pass as expected, I would be able to see them from where I was waiting. Ninety minutes with Sid would give them plenty of time to run to Cobre and follow the railroad south to the highway. Gilbert would be there on a fresh horse to escort them back up the long cedar ridge to Maverick Pass. By the time they hit the pass they should be tuckered out but not for certain. That old gray bell mare was mean and unafraid of a man. If you happened to be in front of her and she wanted to pass, she would almost rather run over you than go around.

I remembered the last spring when we had gathered all of the horses from the mountain save the bell mare and her bunch. I was riding the side holding them along a barbed-wire fence, and in another quarter mile they would be behind a wing fence headed for an open gate to the field. She was in the lead and the Chipmunk stud was next in line. My eyes were mostly on the stud.

The Chipmunk was a beautiful variegated brown, light along the ribcage and on the neck and rump, darker along the back and on his legs. He had a narrow white strip down his face and four white socks about ten inches up his legs. His movement looked effortless. Already I could picture my saddle on him. We were running down the top of an open ridge and I saw the gray bell mare start to lean toward me. She was aware of the trap and was straining every muscle to beat me to the end of the wing fence. I leaned far over in my saddle, riding high in my stirrups and urging my horse to his utmost speed.

We came quickly to the fence. I could see she would hit the end panel and I veered off to the right to avoid the wire, which would break and fly everywhere. I didn't want to be tangled in that mess.

She jumped as she hit the fence and took the top two wires out with her. She must have been watching me because she would have easily cleared the fence had she not jumped so late. I could see blood on her right shoulder as she sped away, not badly hurt considering the possibilities. The Chipmunk stud went behind me and the rest of the bunch filtered through like water running downhill.

Today, with luck, it would be a different story. My big gray horse, Freckles, was fast and I wanted part of the bunch either by a race or on a rope. I didn't care which.

Sid had been in place at the corner of the field only a few minutes when the bunch came through the high pass. The gray bell mare was in the lead as always, domineering, hard-headed matriarch who wouldn't settle for anything short of the lead position. The Chipmunk stud was close behind, only four years old and not yet the real boss of the bunch. The gray mare and stud were about twenty yards out front, the rest in a tight bunch following at full gallop. Rusty then came into view and I could see why the horses were in such tight quarters. My esteem for Rusty went up three notches when I saw him so close. He did a fine job in pushing the horses so fast, though he thought he just had a gentle old bell mare.

Sid got a little extra speed out of the bunch as he headed them on a tour of the flat and I saw Rusty pull up to rest his horse. It would be some time before I would see the horses again. I started Freckles down the ridge, walking him slowly to save his energy, confident my body would warm with some movement. Coming back I skirted the ridge into the draw and found it was much warmer, so I rode up the draw to the top and then climbed the small pinnacle to my observation point. Rusty had disappeared, probably gone back to camp.

I could hear or see nothing of the horses I was waiting for. Several eagles soared high above the granite ledges south of Maverick Pass. Though tiny in the distance, I could hear their screams at intervals when the breeze abated. Their effortless flight always intrigued me. I turned my head quickly at the chatter of a magpie and as I did, Freckles also pricked up his ears and looked. Actually there were three magpies following some deer. I counted four deer: two does and two fawns. Strictly scavengers depending on other animals for their food, magpies often follow deer or coyotes. The deer don't kill anything but they do attract the coyote and cougar. Magpies hope to get a meal from the coyotes or cougars when either makes a kill.

Judging by my shadow, it was just after noon when the horses came through Maverick Pass. Freckles saw them first and I was quick to join him when I noticed his ears come to attention. The gray mare was still in front, Chipmunk next, and the bunch strung out in single file. They were taking it easy and it shouldn't have been that way. Probably something had happened to Gilbert. Maybe his horse fell or lost a shoe or got sick. He would certainly be pushing the horses at a faster pace if he were able.

I waited long enough to pull my cinch tight and for the horses to enter the trails at the head of the long ridge. They saw us as soon as we moved, and the strength they showed when they started to run told me I would have to rope one of them if I was to get a horse that day.

I took my rope down and built a loop as I galloped across the draw. I was still well in lead of them when we came to the trails on the ridge. The gray bell mare was the first one I saw and I immediately raised my rope and waved it back and forth, hollering as loud as I could. She hesitated for just a moment and then I could see she was looking past me toward Independence Valley and Spruce Mountain.

I ran Freckles wide open down the trails, with horses coming alongside on either hand. They were scared to run on the trail with us and were bucking the brush and cedars on either side to pass. I saw the gray mare lunge to avoid a small cedar and race for a clear spot on the ridge just ahead of us. The clearing was about fifty yards long and lined by heavy cedars on the right. I let her pass, though I would have enjoyed choking that obstinate horse's neck for about an hour. It was a near certainty the Chipmunk stud would be following her as he always did. His head came in sight about two long jumps behind her. I shook my loop out clean, and as he came alongside I made a perfect cast. The loop settled close behind his ears and I flipped the rope to draw it tight. The stud was mine—almost.

There was no time to dwell on good fortune. We had already reached the end of the open trail. I dallied the rope four times around the saddle horn as we sped toward a ten-foot tall cedar. It was between us, the rope hitting the tree about four feet off the ground. I had no idea what would happen. What I did know was that if I didn't dally I would lose the rope and the stud. I couldn't just hold the rope in my hand and hope to flip it over the tree.

Time almost stood still; each intricate detail of the next few seconds is still etched in my mind. We were going at full speed—two thousand pounds of horseflesh connected by a mere three-eighths-inch rope. I saw the rope pull through the limbs of the small cedar and I tightened my grasp on my dallies to make ready for the shock I knew would come. The Chipmunk stud was momentarily halted in midair and the rope became taught. He then continued more slowly down the trail. Freckles took the shock much easier because he was the heavier of the two horses, and the leverage was from the saddle horn and not the neck. I chanced a fleeting glance back and saw the tree was uprooted and flying through the air. Spring rains had softened the ground and because of the thin layer of surface soil the roots were close to the top. The tree came out quite easily but not without making me wonder for a moment if the sudden jerk would break my cinch or bring the two horses to a collision point.

The Chipmunk and I fought each other for awhile, but he soon gave up and followed Freckles back to camp where we received a happy welcome. The bell mare and the rest of the bunch circled back toward Holburn Spring instead of going south down the valley. Gilbert's horse had bruised his heel and gone lame, so he was unable to press the horses as planned, and consequently the horses were not played out when they came to me.

The Chipmunk broke out easily and became an excellent cow horse.

The Possum Stud

I was trotting my horse along at a good clip south from the Johnson Ranch toward Little Lake Pass, near where the Western Pacific Railroad crosses the Pequop Range. My tall, willowy, gray horse was shying and snorting at every odd bush and rock along the road. He was looking for an excuse to buck, but it was too cold for me to want any of that extreme exercise so I kept him in close rein. Frosty, as he was called, had measured the length of several cowboys, and was also eager to kick when given the opportunity. I could put up with minor faults like these for a horse that could run and wouldn't fall in every hole or wash. However, the other cowboys warned me that Frosty would get me one day. And he might, but not yet. I always thought that any man who said he hadn't been thrown was the man who rode only gentle horses.

It was early April and rain had been falling for two days. Dark, billowy clouds covered the mountain about halfway down and white, foggy clouds hung close to the valley floor. Gusts of wind made my bat-winged chaps creak and snap. Frosty didn't like that either. He'd look around and snort, then kick at my foot. I galloped him for about a half mile to warm him up and he settled down some.

Somewhere out toward the pass were sixteen mares I wanted to see. They were our work horses used to pull the rakes and mowers during haying time. I wanted to know how many would have colts and if their flesh condition was good enough to carry them through foaling. The tracks on the road indicated that some of them had watered at the ranch spring recently, but not since the rain.

I was certain that the horses would be in the low hills next to the desert or the bald ridges south of the pass. Johnson Mountain is rugged and the only good access trail to the top is from the north. Cougars home up there. While deer are their favorite menu, they are always willing to dine on horseflesh for variety. I saw a two-year-old buckskin come off the mountaintop with a claw track from the top of his back down over his rump—almost a meal for some cougar. Horses that ranged the top of Johnson Mountain were always skittish, spooking at every strange movement. I thought they must live in daily fear.

I left the road where it made a bend toward Shafter and rode on a wide trail toward the pass. In a few minutes I came to Rock Spring Wash and found eight of the mares grazing near the water. There were many horse tracks pointed toward the pass and I followed them. I was not really trying to track them, rather just going in the same direction.

About two miles ahead of me a high, bald peak towered above the lower hills, and I headed for it knowing I could see most of the range country from there. I climbed the east side of the peak, partially sheltered from the brisk wind coming straight from the west. The hill was steep and I rested Frosty several times before reaching the crest. When I rode out on top I saw Independence Valley was filled with a white, rolling fog. There were three unknown horses directly below me and I recognized the rest of the work mares on the west side of the divide. Almost as I saw the work mares the fog rolled up the pass and swallowed them.

I directed my attention to the three horses a short distance below. They were all dark in color, either dark brown or black. I didn't know them by sight, mine being the only branded horses in the area. There were mustangs scattered over the range to the south and in the valley east, as well as west. In fact, as I looked at the desert toward Black Point I could see many horses. They looked like little spots of pepper against the light background.

One of the horses arched his neck and pranced around the other two, and I was sure he was a young stud and the other two were his mares. The blanket of fog began to roll through the pass and climb higher on the hills.

Soon the mustangs disappeared under a mass of billowing, rolling fog. It crept up the peak until just the tiny spot where I was standing was clear. Frosty turned and squirmed, wanting to run or buck or do something to relieve his pent-up energy. It was scary up there on that tiny island, not able to see any other land. The whole world had dropped out from under us and we were left floating. The wind whipped my chaps and Frosty spun one way and then the other to get away from them. Finally, by facing the wind I calmed him down slightly; however, I sensed that he would bolt if given half a chance.

It took several minutes for the wind to blow the fog through the pass, but when it did, the sun was clear and almost warm and the cold wind subsided considerably. All the clouds disappeared except for those capping Johnson Mountain.

The three dark horses were indeed mustangs, a stud and two mares, and the best thing to do would be to add the gentle mares to the stud's harem. If he accepted them I might possibly ease them to the ranch over the next few days. If I could be patient and not scare him clear away, I would have a good chance.

I kept out of sight of the mustangs and went down around the mares. They were all gentle and gave me no trouble at all as I drove them to the mustangs. The dark brown stud came out to meet them with a defiant arch in his neck and his front hooves stepping high. There was no stud to challenge him as one by one he greeted the mares, accepting them with a snort and a thump of his right hoof. After they had all been officially welcomed he pranced around, head and tail high, defying any and all to do battle with him.

It took about an hour for him to go through all of his rituals and calm down enough to allow his greatly increased harem to graze. By this time the fog had rolled across the Steptoe Valley and disappeared toward the Great Salt Lake. The sun was warming and it was almost a decent day. I started to plot my strategy.

Oh, the excitement of it, the glamour, the romance of being a cowboy. How thrilling to ride with the rancher's daughter across the green meadows where there are no deerflies or mosquitoes or greenheads—just the sunshine and birds singing near the brook. Then every evening to play the guitar and wail lonely tunes to her as you listen to the crickets and the frogs. I thought a few moments of the many illusions surrounding the cowboy. Then I thought again of the romance. Today and maybe for several days I was going to play that part to the very hilt, and if I was victorious, soon that brown stud would be romanced into captivity and looking out from under me as we rode with some rancher's daughter out on the range.

I decided I would just show myself. Not ride toward the mustangs but cross where they could see me and then ride away. Sort of a cat-and-mouse game: now I'm here and now I'm gone. In some way I had to get all of the horses accustomed to me so I could lure them, in some fashion, toward the ranch, and quietly ease them into the lower field. Tonight I would open the gate so it would be ready to accept the horses.

The horses saw me as soon as I came in sight, and the brown stud pranced out toward me a few steps expecting to meet a challenger. When he determined that it was not another stud he spun away toward the mares, drove them into a close bunch, and then whistled and danced away on the opposite side from me. I rode back out of sight and waited. He soon came back, very nervous but reluctant to leave the mares.

Several times I played the same game that afternoon, always showing up on the side away from the ranch, so the movement that was made brought us a few feet—a few yards—closer to the ranch. The gentle mares were quiet and cooperative each time and the two wild mares soon stayed in the center of the bunch for protection. The stud continued to be cagey, arrogant, and distrusting, and time after time I was sure he had left for good. However when I was about to give him up for lost, I would hear his familiar whinney and he would trot back to the mares.

By this method I gradually moved the horses down into the low hills not far from the Rock Spring where I thought they would water if I left them for the night. The sun was just going out of sight behind the crest of Johnson Mountain and the cooler evening air made me shiver. This surely would be the ideal time to leave. I divined that if the horses did move it would be early in the morning, and maybe they would come in and water before going back to the hills. Frosty was cold and nervous from just watching the horses all day and was anxious to gallop, so I loosed the reins and let him go. It took only a few minutes to travel the five or six miles to the ranch.

Early the next morning I was out there again with the horses. They were all together and, as I expected, were trailing in to water. The stud was a little reluctant but followed along. I rode wide around them so as not to excite the stud. I was riding Freckles, another gray horse. This, I thought, would not break the pattern the stud had seen the day before: a man on a gray horse quietly following along when they moved, and just sitting out there when they grazed.

I had moved the stud off his home range. The trails were unfamiliar, the hills different. He would know the direction of his range, but he was more inclined to follow than to lead. The mares drank at the spring and continued toward the ranch. In a few minutes they came to the other eight mares and it was interesting to watch the stud accept them into his bunch. His desires for the mares became stronger and he followed along, at times even in the center of the bunch.

It was not much past noon when the mares decided to go into the ranch, which was only a couple of miles away. They quit grazing one by one, and when one of the old mares nickered they walked to the road and started jogging toward the ranch and that open gate. I held back, not wanting to stir the stud or cause any excitement that would turn him back to the hills.

I smiled as I watched the bunch start through the gate. The brown stud was in the middle of the horses and he paused at the gate, but when other horses passed him and went inside, he did also. I followed along and closed the gate. After a few days for the horses to get used to the fences and surroundings I decided to try for the capture. I spread several piles of hay around in the corral so the mares wouldn't hesitate at the gate, and with riders about fifty yards down the lane on either side of the corral gate for security, I brought them in. By this time the stud was well acquainted with the mares and followed willingly into the corral.

I named him Possum. He was six years old and short coupled, with a fiery but kind disposition, a well-muscled body, and clean legs. My saddle covered his back from withers to hip. He became an excellent cow horse and was still in the cavy at age fifteen.

Gray Eagle

My 2:00 to 4:00 A.M. herding tour was just coming to an end and I could hear the crew of ten cowboys riding out from the chuck wagon. It was the first week in August and the Wine Cup cow outfit was making a beef drive to the Gallaher pasture. We had gathered 826 two-year-old beef steers during the last three weeks and today we would put them on the tall, lush grass of Gallaher to finish them out. The herd was resting quietly on an almost level sagebrush bench about a half mile north of the Eccles Ranch, only six miles from the pasture.

When I watched the cowboys get the cattle up and start them on the trail, I felt some misgivings. This night herding I had just finished would be my last with the Wine Cup until next spring. I was going to run a few wild horses. Some of the boys said I was crazy and that I had no chance at all of making any money. Then there were others who indicated they would even like to go with me. To heck with the money, it would be an exciting adventure. My boss was reluctant to see me go and made me promise to stay with them long enough to see this drive completed, which was today. There was only a scattering of steers left to gather, so I didn't feel that I was leaving them shorthanded.

I was anxious to get back to my small farmstead on Grouse Creek and look at my horses again. Maybe break a few, haul a little wood for winter, and try to rope a few mustangs. A week ago I had seen the mustang stud from Nine Mile Mountain that we called the Gray Eagle. He and his bunch were watering in the early dawn where Burnt Creek comes into Thousand Springs Creek about a mile above the Eccles Ranch. Since then my thoughts had continually strayed back to him, a beautiful freckled gray that always saw you first, a horse with an eagle eye—hence his name—Gray Eagle.

During many of my lonesome hours while trailing cattle I daydreamed of him, concocting various ideas of how I might capture him. Today I was going to try one of those plans.

I jogged my horse slowly back to camp and turned him loose. My big red sorrel was standing near the entrance to the rope corral looking out and he nickered as I approached. I spoke to him quietly in loving tones we both understood as I gently placed the bridle on him. Ed, our nighthawk, came out from breakfast just at that moment.

"Gonna ride that old crow bait again?" he queried. Ed was a rough talker, but he was the kindest man with horses I have ever seen. He joked with me often but was always a good friend when I needed him.

"Sure, Ed, thought I'd put a few slow miles on him. He's gettin' fat as a pig. You must be putting him on the best grass every night."

"I do, but not because of you. It's because he's such a good horse and he has to put up with the likes of you. I feel real sorry for him, real sorry." Ed always tried hard not to say anything about me that could be misunderstood for praise. He was an incessant tease.

"I'm goin' out on Nine Mile Mountain to rope the Gray Eagle today, and tomorrow I'll neck him to my black horse and take him home. Throw my bedroll off at the Gamble Ranch will you, Ed, and I'll drive the old jalopy down later and haul the roll home."

"Sure will, Parley," he said. Then his attitude changed to excitement. "Say, I saw that gray stud and his bunch this morning. They were watering just below the Eccles field."

"Are you sure, Ed? It was still quite dark when you were out there." I wanted to believe him but didn't want to build up hopes on a guess.

"It was him all right. The moon was up enough so I could see pretty good. There were eleven of them coming off the Nine Mile side to water. The old white mare is still with them and there are three colts. Now do you think I saw them?"

I could tell by his earnest expression that he was telling me the truth. I wanted a chance at that stud and this would be a wonderful opportunity.

"You've convinced me, Ed." The beat of my heart advanced a few strokes just to think of that wild rascal. "I'm sure gonna try him, Ed. Thanks. I'll see you tonight." I turned and went to the chuck wagon for breakfast. Ed waved his hand as he ambled toward his saddle horse. In a few minutes I was eating and Ed had the saddle horses headed out to graze. Ed was born with one leg shorter than the other and couldn't perform all of the duties of a cowboy, but he could ride a gentle horse and do the nighthawking, the herding of saddle horses at night. Sometimes this meant watching them for part of the day as well. Four hours of sleep is a good average night for a cowboy in the summertime—at least in this outfit. And that's usually what Ed got.

I ate my breakfast of steak, hot biscuits, and gravy, thanking the cook for the tasty meal. The two hours on night watch had reduced my supper to nothing and my stomach was wondering if my throat had been cut. The steak soon relieved the hunger pangs, and I also took a good drink of icy water because I didn't know when I would have a chance to drink again. I wasn't carrying any water with me.

I threw my Hamley saddle on Goldie, turned him around a couple of times to loosen him up, and stepped up into his middle. Goldie hogged a couple of short jumps without lowering his head and then walked away with a hump in his back that would make a camel proud. I knew with him acting so impish that his rest had been sufficient and he was ready to go to work.

Based on what Ed had told me, that the stud had come in to water directly below the Eccles field, I guessed the horses would go back out on the same trails they came in on or no farther away than the next ridge. They would follow the trails out for a short distance and then graze the sagebrush draws and ridges back toward Nine Mile Mountain, if my intuition was correct. I could go out through the lane above the Eccles Ranch and travel a long, low ridge toward the mountain, having a higher ridge between me and the mustangs. This, I decided, was my best chance to get in front of them where I wanted to be. A slight breeze was coming from the north and east and would reveal my presence if I should follow directly in the path of the horses.

I traveled slowly but persistently, jogging short distances when the terrain allowed, until I came to a point near the mountain that I thought would place Goldie and me well ahead of the horses. The brush and a few cedar trees were intermingled, and we wound our way between them as we angled back along the side of the ridge.

We came out on top, but no horses were in sight. I dismounted and left Goldie standing while I walked to an abutment of rocks. Looking from them I could see the entire area below me, close in and far out. Possibly the horses had crossed the ridge back of me. I decided to wait and see if they would come from one of the cedar-covered draws below where I was watching.

I patted Goldie on the neck and rubbed my hand down his heavily muscled foreleg. He was a great horse—gentle, clean of limb, well muscled, and an eager competitor on the rope. Each time I took my rope down to build a loop he would perk up and start looking for something to run after. Whether a calf, a horse, a coyote, or a rabbit, he was ready to do his best. I walked back along his side and ran my hand across his smooth flank. Goldie is the only horse I have ever seen that has no curl in his flank hair. It lays back along his side and straight across the flank, a unique marking.

I felt Goldie move and saw that he was looking intently at something. I supposed it would be the horses but it could be something else. Quietly I walked up in front of him so I could see much of the area below. It was Gray Eagle and his bunch. The commotion that attracted Goldie was the stallion chasing one of the mares to put her in place. Evidently she grazed away in the wrong direction or was too slow to catch up. In any case she was properly chastised and went back among the horses bunched near a thick grove of cedars on the rim of a long draw.

I considered the stud might want the mares to rest in the shade for awhile, but if he did, his attitude changed because the entire bunch started grazing across the open sage flat toward me. The stud was stirred up and nervous, continually trotting out of the bunch to challenge an unseen enemy. I was quite certain he hadn't seen me, yet his actions were such that he must have some intuition of impending danger. The stud stopped by a large cedar that stood alone in the clearing and went through the ritual of depositing dung on the stud pile to let all know he was accepting the challenge from any source.

I loosened my cinches, shook my saddle into place, and tightened them again for roping. Goldie looked around and rattled his nose with a big sigh. I think he knew what was about to happen. I led Goldie back from the observation point, mounted, unfastened my rope, and, holding to the knot end, tossed it full length out in front of me to get the kinks out of it. Carefully I collected it in neat coils and built a loop I thought was just the right size for good balance. I brought this loop up in an extra coil and held it all in my right hand. Several times I dropped the loop coil to see if it would shake loose without a twist. I certainly didn't want to have a chance to catch Gray Eagle only to find a twist in the loop.

I felt Goldie come tense under me as I worked with the rope, and I was sure he would do his part, whatever it might be. Goldie and I traversed the hill around to the left, avoiding the brush areas and the rocks that might kick loose and startle the horses. We came to a saddle pass between the high lookout ridge and Nine Mile Mountain and saw there was a deep, cedar-filled draw that would take me directly to the horses.

In my mind I marked a big, dry cedar which stood high on the right side of the draw as a place to stop and make my final plans. It was almost directly opposite the bunch of mustangs.

My plan was to take advantage of the stallion's nervousness. His instincts told him danger was near and made him alert as he guarded his harem. Often he trotted away from the bunch and listened for a sign of danger, and that would be when I would make my move. When he was away on one of these trips, his rump toward me, I would charge out from the cedars directly toward his mares. I divined that he might see Goldie as another stallion trying to take his mares and, without hesitation, come charging to meet the challenge. I would be lying low along Goldie's neck, partially blocked from view by his head as he ran. Just at the right moment I would rise up in the saddle, swing my rope once or twice, and cast the loop. If he whirled away as I threw it, it was my expectation he would turn to the right toward his mares. In my mind I could see exactly how it would happen.

We went carefully down the draw, staying to the softer soils to muffle Goldie's footsteps, making as little sound as possible. We came to the dry tree and I reined Goldie to the left between some large cedar trees. We climbed just high enough out of the draw for me to see the mustangs. They showed no special signs of fear and I knew we had made it that far without being detected. I shook my loop out and watched it fall clean without any kinks. I was pleased and gathered it up again. The stud was trotting off from the herd, angling to the right and away from me. I judged that I was about a hundred yards from the mares. When the stud stopped this time I would go.

I suddenly gave Goldie the reins and we shot forward out of the grove at full gallop. I was laying low over his neck and could hear only the pounding of hooves and the breaking of brush as Goldie charged straight toward the mares.

Time almost stopped, for I saw all of these things in the next few seconds: the mares saw us first and formed into a tight bunch, and the stud turned immediately and aimed his attack directly at me. This was exactly what I wanted him to do. With ears laid back and teeth showing in frenzied hate, he hurled himself toward me in giant strides.

For just a moment a fear came over me. What if Gray Eagle didn't stop when I rose up? Maybe he would complete his challenge and strike me from the saddle with flailing hooves. I had seen studs fight and knew their instruments of war were very effective.

Two more strides—one more—now! I rose up and shook my loop out, flipping it up round my head as I did. I could hear the swish of the seagrass rope in the air. At once the wild stud slid to a dusty stop, surprise showing in his eyes. He scrambled to turn in midair, and as he effected his change of direction the rope whisked a second time, I cast it over his head, and he hit the ground broadside to me. With a deft flip I closed the noose just behind his ears and quickly put three dallies around the saddle horn. I had him on a short rope, and although he fought courageously and hard, he gave in and I took him back to the cow wagon still camped near the Eccles Ranch.

When I saw Ed, he said, "I thought you might get him today. Just a hunch, I guess."

Gray Eagle broke to be most gentle, although he liked to buck a little after a short rest. He was seven years old and filled out to weigh just under a thousand pounds. Sometimes I wonder what I would have done had he continued his charge toward me.

Water Trap

Four of my friends and I decided to try water trapping some mustangs. It was the middle of September and the weather was dry and had been for the last six weeks. If it would stay dry for another month, we would have just the kind of weather needed to set up a good water trap.

There were about two hundred mustangs on Delno Mountain and no live springs there where they could drink. The few small springs where some of the horses normally watered were dry, forcing them to go to one of four places: Crittenden Spring located in the canyon east of the mountain; Eighteen Mile Spring at the base of the mountain to the south; above Eighteen Mile Ranch on Thousand Springs Creek; or Rock Spring Wash. Here water would run on top of the ground for a ways in the wash and then sink, only to rise again a distance down the wash. Rock Spring Wash is where most of the horses would normally go for water.

Rock Spring Wash is about six miles long but has water in it for only about two miles. The wash is probably eighty feet wide in some places, the sides about six to twenty feet high and in many places straight up like a wall. There are spots where small floods have washed in from the mountains to the east, and the wild horses have taken advantage of this by sliding down these gullies to water, making several deeply cut trails into the wash. There are, however, distances hundreds of feet long where there is a wall on both sides from ten to twenty feet high without a break.

We planned to direct many of the horses to Rock Spring Wash by flagging the spring below Eighteen Mile Ranch and the short strip of Thousand Springs Creek where the horses could water above the ranch. We knew it would take too much work to flag Crittenden Spring. Our biggest problem would be to keep the mustangs from drinking in Rock Spring Wash until they were dry enough to come in where we wanted them, where we had a trap corral to hold them.

This was all casual planning at first, but as the days went by we became more serious, and then someone suggested we should string binder twine across the top of the higher bushes and use sheets of paper tied along the string for the flags. Binder twine is a coarse-fibered string used to tie grain bundles on the old grain binding machines.

The distance from home to where we would camp was about seventy miles by road, and it took a full week to haul two loads of hay, camping equipment, and materials to build the trap corral. We picked a campsite where a wide tributary entered the main wash and where there was running water for our use. Each of us took two saddle horses which we trailed across the mountain about thirty miles as the crow flies.

We worked from daylight until dark each day preparing for the horses. No one had a watch so we used the morning star for our morning indicator, figuring it came up about 4:00 A.M. In the course of two days we built two fences across the wash and effected the trap corral. One fence was solid and the other we put in a narrow place so we could close it off with a long gate. This gate would open against the wall of the wash and the horses would be less likely to see it when they came in the night to water.

The next few days we strung our twine and flagged it, starting at Eighteen Mile Spring and working toward camp. In three days we noticed a significant influx of horses in our area. The flags moving with every breath of air effectively scared the horses away from the water and we were pleased at the thought of what we might accomplish.

Most of the horses had started using the deep trails close to our camp to slide down into the wash where they would water and then go back toward the mountain. I noticed the many different temperaments of the individual horses. One older stud came down to the flagged twine, jumped over it, and went in to drink. When he was finished he came back, jumped the twine, and walked away like he owned the whole country. Others stayed far from the twine, apparently scared of the dangling paper fluttering with every slight breeze.

We had to constantly ride the flagged line to keep the horses back and some still broke through at night. I roped a three-year-old palomino stud hanging around the flag line. I came up on him unexpectedly and when he ran toward his bunch I cut corners and caught him.

The sixth day we closed all the deep trails with large sagebrush except two that let the horses enter where our corral was located. Late in the evening we opened the trail. One man on horseback stayed there until dark to keep horses from entering too early.

When dark finally came two of us went down into the wash on foot, advanced to the open gate, and crawled back into a small cave we had fashioned in the wall of the wash. On the way down into the wash we made sure the two trails were free from all brush. There were two of us because the gate was heavy and we wanted to be certain we could move it fast enough to close and lock it before the horses stampeded. In the dark they would run over anything—including us.

About an hour passed and no sign of the horses. The time went on and on, and we were cramped and cold. It was cold enough that ice formed along the stream each night, and this night was no exception.

I squirmed a little, and my companion pressed my arm. We both listened intently. They were coming. Which ones and how many didn't matter; they were coming. Our cold bodies were stiff and shaking, partly from the thrill and excitement and partly from the cold.

The horses came closer, snorted, and turned back. They milled around for a short time and came close again. This time one of the braver ones walked through the gate and trotted the hundred or so feet to the water. The rest of the bunch soon followed. In my mind I counted three—four—a small group went through—maybe three or four more. Several others followed until I wondered if the corral would hold them all. I expected the first ones in might soon be getting their fill of water and want to leave.

We stayed a little longer and two more bunches came in. They quickly trotted to the water where the others were drinking and nervously milling around. I patted my buddy and we rolled out of the cave and raced across the wash, carrying the end of the gate as we rushed to close and lock it.

I snapped the chain together at the bottom and he fastened the top as prearranged. The gate was nine feet high and made of strong poles. We hoped all the horses would not hit it at the same time and put a terrific weight on the long panels. We braced the gate in three places with short poles we had prepared for this purpose and went back down the wash so the horses couldn't see or smell us. We hoped they would quiet down; however, we could still hear them moving around as we climbed out on top.

There were at least four older studs in the trap, and it would be some time before they would settle down. Maybe they would churn all night.

I was sweating from the exertion, my heart pounding at a terrific pace. That was tremulous excitement, complete accomplishment making the body tremble, shiver, and throb—and sweat, in spite of the cold. There is nothing that can compare with that feeling.

We ran the several yards to camp and were met by our buddies. "What happened?" came at us from all three simultaneously, and we answered in unison, "We've got 'em!"

Normally it doesn't take long to stay all night from dark until 4:00 A.M., but this night, though a good part of it was used, hung on interminably. None of us slept more than a few minutes. Question after question was asked: What was it like when they came in? How many did we have? Did we think the gate would hold? What color are they? The answers were vague, guesses mostly. Neither of us could be certain of anything except that we had some wild mustangs in the corral and would see them when daylight came and if the corral held.

When we thought daylight was coming, we broke the ice on the stream and made ready for breakfast. Our saddle horses ate their oats while we had fried spuds and a couple of eggs with a wide strip of sow belly, something akin to home-cured bacon. It sure tasted good, and I think after eating that nice breakfast, I could have gone right to sleep.

I looked at the eastern horizon when I went out to take the nose bags off the horses and, sure enough, there was the morning star just peeping over the crest of Round Top, a smooth peak on the side of Delno. I laughed and called the others out to look. We all agreed it was the morning star, big and bright. We must have arisen near to 2:00 A.M.

Morning came and we saddled our horses. A man on horseback would be much less scary to the wild horses. After all, we had ridden through, around, and among them for days. They should be somewhat accustomed to us by now.

We rode to a point below the corral so we could look into the wash where the horses were trapped. Each man counted once, twice. The horses milled and crowded each other until it was difficult to be certain just how many we did have in the corral. Finally we agreed there were at least nineteen. Not one of us was positive as to the exact number.

When we rode to a closer observation point, I noticed a red roan stud. I could tell by his heavy neck and jaw that he was a stud, and he kept circling the corral looking at the walls of the embankment. He trotted nervously around several times like a high jumper eyeing the bar, then with just a few quick strides he lunged at the dirt wall. His feet churned rapidly as foot by foot he climbed that almost perpendicular wall. He came out on the far side of the wash from us and got away.

What a dandy saddle horse he would have been. Others tried to do the same but fell back into the wash. They just didn't have the strength and desire of the roan stud.

We had eighteen horses when we finally made a good count. Each of us picked a young stud to break for riding. We kept the best of the other young animals to take home, and the old ones were sold for what we considered chicken feed—about six dollars each.

We did catch several more over the next few days, but they were mostly older animals. I thought I might freeze to death before we finished the water trapping expedition, but I lived through it to remember those thrilling moments.

The Phantom's Yearling

I awoke sometime in the night to the sound of rain pattering on my canvas bed tarp and tenderly inspected its perimeter to make certain no water was entering. The evening before when I picked the spot to roll out my bed I was careful to choose a gravel swell with a slight slope. Dark clouds were closing in and it looked like rain might fall before morning. I was always one to prepare for the worst and hope for the best. I sleepily reminded myself that the ditch around my bed was adequate and there was almost no chance that rain could run under my bed and swamp me. I was never a boy scout, but a couple of years' experience rolling my bed out on the ground gradually taught me a few things.

Gently I pushed up the rain-soaked tarp where it covered my face to give me more breathing space. I was careful not to touch its treated surface because it might leak if rubbed when wet on the outside. I would be damp enough by morning without tempting water to come through my cover. After these few checks and adjustments I snuggled a little deeper into bed and tried to go back to sleep. The cool, moist, fresh air was conducive to sleep, but by then my mind was alert and recalling some happenings of the last few weeks. I intentionally skipped over everyday work experiences, but I remembered fondly the night of the St. Patrick's dance.

I rode in from the ranch with Ed in his brown Chevy roadster, and he let me borrow the car to pick up my girlfriend, Bell. I didn't ask Ed. He just said right out of the blue sky, "Here's my keys. Take the jalopy and pick up your gal." That Ed is sure a good one to have for a friend.

Bell and I danced the night away, and when I left her at her door at 4:00 A.M., she asked when I might come in again. I knew better, but I said I'd see her to the May Day dance. We made a date and I promised to be there for certain. Now here I was, three long days' ride from town, and the dance only a week away. Talk about being a romantic cowboy, I was one all right, but my work was sure giving me some competition. We were going to be out here four days chasing mustangs; that would leave three days to return for the dance. Maybe I would make it, just maybe.

I don't know how long I lay there daydreaming, so to speak, but when I peeked out again it was coming daylight. I glanced toward the cabin nearby and couldn't see a light, so I figured breakfast was not ready yet.

The rain had dwindled away to just a few small drops, not enough to soak a person, but still damp. I reached under the edge of my bed tarp near my pillow and brought forth my small Stetson hat, shaped it to fit my liking, and eased it gently onto my head. It would be several minutes before the hat would be warm enough to be comfortable. It was the first item I put on and already I sort of felt dressed. I pulled my socks from under my pillow and, after shaking them out, I put them on my feet. They were warm but damp. My shirt was also damp, as were my trousers. Maybe they would dry some from body warmth, maybe not. I turned my boots upside down and shook them vigorously to dislodge any rodent that might have used them as shelter from the storm. Nothing came out, so I pulled them on, strapped my spurs in place, and as I stood up I brought my coat with me. I folded my bed under the tarp and gave it a glance—I was sure it would be just as wet when I came back to sleep in it again that night.

As I went toward the corral, intent on graining the horses before breakfast, I heard Sid call from the open cabin door, "Rise and shine. Breakfast in ten minutes." The rise part I could do, but that shine part was another thing. The ten minutes I knew meant thirty minutes, or whenever I happened to get the horses cared for and returned to the cabin.

I hung the nose bags on the horses for them to eat their ration of oats and threw them some fresh hay. When I checked the water in the trough it was low, so I started the gas engine that ran the pump. Leaving the pumphouse I heard the nicker of old Smut, my gray saddle horse, and I knew he had finished his oats. As I took the bag from his head, I patted him on the neck and promised him a long, hard run that day. He rattled a big sigh and turned toward the fresh hay.

In a few more minutes I had finished my chores and headed for breakfast. It was broad daylight by then and the rain had stopped. My saddle lay on its side near the cabin door, with my bat-winged chaps draped over to protect it from the rain. I picked up the chaps and buckled them on, thinking they might as well be warming up as I ate.

Hot sourdough biscuits are good anytime and especially early on a chilly morning such as this one. Four slices of bacon and two eggs with their eyes closed were shuffled from the hotcake turner to my plate, and I was ready to eat.

Between bites of food I chanced a subtle question at Sid. "Do you think we will be back at the H-D by Friday?"

"What's today?" he asked.

"Friday, I think. I mean by next Friday so we can go to the dance."

He shot me a quizzical look. "You courtin' some young female?"

"Ya, but not very often. You guys keep me too far from town."

Gilbert, my other partner, chuckled a little. "Why don't you wait a couple years 'til you grow up and then I'll take you to town. Better than chasin' those high school gals. Safer too." Gilbert wasn't looking for a wife and I knew it.

"I'll think about it, Gilbert, but in the meantime I'd like to go the May Day dance. I sort of promised a lovely lady I'd be there."

"You ought to know not to make promises," Sid said, and that ended the conversation. I knew if I could just get to the H-D Ranch I could ride to town with Ed again. He always went to the dances.

We saddled our horses—Gilbert his big white gelding he loved so much, Sid a bay standard-bred horse he called Dan, and I saddled Smut. Those three horses should be able to run any mustang into submission if we had good luck starting them. Gilbert and Sid rode side by side toward the finger-like ridges running from the Toana range west to Steptoe Valley. Dan was a little string-halt in his left hind leg, and I thought he was jerking his foot extra high, maybe because of the cool, wet weather. He would get better as he warmed up, and it didn't seem to hurt his running anyway. I trotted my horse along behind, content to be alone with my thoughts.

My mind focused back on the ride's purpose. We were out to capture a bunch of gray mustangs. They were led by a white stallion, though some who had been close said his skin was black under the white hair, because his nose and eyes showed black and he had black hooves. I didn't know, I had only seen him once, and then at some distance. He was a pretty sight and I could understand why he was called the Phantom. As white as he was, his body would disappear before your eyes in the heat waves and mirages of the desert.

One story claimed that the Phantom was an Arabian stud, brought to the desert by an old horse runner who was going to use the stallion to lead the mares into a trap corral he built. His plan was to shoot the monarch stud and turn the Phantom loose with the bunch. Then he would gain control of the mares and lead them into the corral.

Some of this could be true but not all, because the horses were still on the range as wild and free as ever, and the horse runner was only mentioned in tales told by the old-timers and drunks who were known to make up stories and exaggerate. I had never seen the trap corral, nor had either of the two with me. Yet the white stud was out there somewhere on those gravel ridges. There were nine horses in the bunch, all gray when young, turning white like the Phantom as they matured.

Gilbert pulled his horse up at the base of a long ridge and I rode up beside him.

"Do you think Old Chalk came out of the Phantom's bunch, Gilbert? He's white with black skin and hooves."

"No, I don't think so. Old Chalk was mothered by the old wild bell mare up on Squaw Creek. I don't know who his sire was. Probably some mustang stud over in Independence Valley." Gilbert patted Old Chalk on the neck. "He's a great horse, must have had a good sire."

Gilbert chuckled to himself a little as he often did and slapped the end of his leather reins on the pommel of his saddle. He squinted from under his gray fedora and told us a more logical story about how the Phantom probably came into this area.

"Ya know, down south of here in the Deep Creek country there are a lot of white horses. Bunches of them. They have black skins, are born smut colored and then as they get older they turn gray and then white. They are good-looking horses; many of them could be mistaken for Arabians. They have fine features and small, refined heads. I've heard all these barroom tales about this horse we call the Phantom but I think he's a stud from the Deep Creek Country. He probably ran off from some mustanger down there or maybe even followed a bunch of wintering mares back this way in the spring. He's a fine looking horse, and I would like to get hold of him regardless of where he came from."

That was perhaps the longest conversation Gilbert ever made. He was not one to make up stories or multiply words. He shifted in his saddle and said thoughtfully, "Parley, you always have good luck starting a bunch. Why don't you go down the flat and bring them back to us? Sid could stay right along here somewhere and I'll go up into Silver Zone country. Maybe I could wait near the trails that come off Toana Mountain just south of the pass. I've seen the Phantom and his bunch several times near that heavy cedar ridge just past the deep canyon."

He pointed to the area and I knew exactly where he meant. That was where I saw the Phantom that stormy day last spring. I ran the horses several miles that day and then watched them climb a ridge toward the mountain about where we were sitting at the moment. Last spring my horse played out and I couldn't turn the Phantom and his bunch back toward the desert where Sid was waiting with a fresh horse. Today Sid would be near where we now sat on our horses. All I had to do was get the mustangs to run the same route as last spring, and Sid would take them to Silver Zone Pass. Gilbert would be waiting there, and he was sure he could run them across the valley to the Johnson Ranch.

"I'll be here about noon with the horses," I said confidently, though I knew it was a long shot to even think of bringing the horses to a prearranged place.

"I'll be on that little knoll among the cedars," Sid said, pointing to a small hump on the ridge south of us. That was fine with me, so I reined Smut in a southerly direction and rode away.

A thunderhead passed over me, bringing a cold, hard-driven rain. I was glad just the edge of it caught me, as the center of the squall was a hailstorm that left the ground covered a full inch deep. Other squalls and black thunderheads dotted the country around me. Any of them could leave rain or hail on the ground as this one had.

Smut and I trotted south past the ends of the gravel ridges, following a trail part of the way and picking our way through the short sagebrush when no trail was visible. I searched each draw as we went past, looking especially close at the patches of cedars for white horses, any white horses. White shouldn't be hard to locate. I saw three bunches of horses, but no grays or whites. The sun peeked through the cloud-filled sky only now and then, yet I was completely warm. Smut's jogging movement kept my blood circulating sufficiently to make even my feet warm in my wet boots.

I skirted the ridge to my left, climbing a little to bring me to a higher plane in the deep draw. From there I climbed the face of the south ridge and aimed at a jut of rocks on the crest of the ridge. I would be able to see distances much easier from there than from a lower level.

Smut picked his way gently through the sharp, jagged rocks, hesitating when there seemed to be no clear place to place his foot. I watched him carefully, riding easy in my stirrups in case he should fall. I wanted every chance possible to clear myself should this happen, but

Smut was as sure footed as a goat and brought us out on top without mishap.

I dismounted and checked his feet to see if he had cut or bruised them and was pleased to see he was all right. As soon as I had reset my saddle, I tied Smut to a tree limb and walked out on the edge of the rocks to observe the area. A happy, excited feeling came to me as I looked at the white horses about two hundred yards down the ridge from me. It was the bunch I wanted and they were lounging around in a small grove of cedar trees completely unaware of my presence. I was glad that I had climbed to the rocks, because my former course would have taken me directly to the horses and probably started them south instead of north toward Silver Zone. Smut and I rested a few minutes while I scrutinized the terrain we were about to cross. I could see no washes large enough to bother, and if I was able to start the Phantom the way I wanted it would be easy running, maybe the full five miles back to Sid.

Smut and I approached the mustangs from the south, and as soon as they started to run we turned toward the desert and went down the crest of that ridge at full gallop, grateful there were no obstructions to slow us down. We traveled about a half mile into the desert before I could see the horses coming out of the deep draw. They were headed for the desert floor as I had guessed they would be, but I was so far ahead that it surprised them and they halted their headlong race and gathered in a tight bunch to adjust to the new situation. A big, white mare trotted toward me, followed by the Phantom stud, who passed her and came on until he was only about a hundred yards from where I sat.

What a magnificent animal he was, his beautifully refined head held high in challenge and defiance. His body was thick for a mustang, his legs were clean, and as near as I could see he had no blemishes.

The Phantom blew a loud whistle at me and it was followed by one from the white mare. They whirled in unison and headed north on the trails toward Silver Zone Pass, the mare taking the lead and trying to bounce like a deer for a few jumps. She soon settled down to a gallop while the stud gathered up his harem and followed. The race was on.

Smut and I stayed close enough to keep them running, and when they got lined out I counted twelve head. Three were smaller and probably yearlings; their coats were a darker color than the older animals.

Sid was in just the right place and took them on toward Gilbert and Silver Zone Pass. I stopped chasing the mustangs and rested Smut for several minutes, moving him around so he wouldn't cool off too fast and

get stiff. After awhile I walked him to the top of the small knoll where
Sid had waited. From there I could see the flat bench west of Silver Zone
Pass where the horses would cross if Gilbert could turn them toward the
ranch. A squally rain soaked me thoroughly before it turned into small
pellets of ice that stung my face and made Smut turn his rump toward it
in disgust. It was soon over, however, and I shook my chaps and rope to
dislodge the pockets of snow and ice before they could melt and
penetrate. My seagrass rope was already so saturated that it bounced
like a coil of wire.

While I sat absorbed in my own thoughts, wondering if I should stay
or ride back to camp, I heard a horse coming down the opposite slope
from me. It was one of those darker yearlings. Smut saw the mustang
and whinnied to it. The yearling stopped, answered back, and came
toward me at a trot. I couldn't understand what Smut was telling the
yearling each time he nickered but it must have been something he
wanted to hear because the mustang, without regard toward me, came
up and smelled Smut's nose, then opened his mouth and chawed the air
expecting a reprimand of some kind. I was fascinated as I watched the
two of them become friends, all the time wondering how I could get that
stiff rope around the yearling's neck. If I swung the rope it would scare
the yearling away and spoil all of the coaxing Smut had done to get the
yearling close in the first place.

I decided to trail along at a walk toward camp and figure what might
be best to do. I knew the yearling would not stay with me and follow
into the many strange things around camp. Out here I was the only
strange thing and Smut had already told the yearling I was all right. We
went slowly toward the cabin, the mustang following so close his head
was almost touching Smut's tail. Every few minutes he would nicker and
Smut would answer. Often during the first mile the yearling would raise
his head and look for the other horses of his bunch, but not seeing them
he was content to stay with his new friend.

We went along about another mile and I knew I must try something.
I loosed my rope from its strap and built a loop I thought to be just the
right size for the yearling's delicate head. Not so big that he might go
through it, but not so small that it would be hard to throw. Gradually I
moved the rope around, holding it in my hand, flipping it just a little
and moving it back and forth so the yearling might become used to it
and not be too startled when I cast the loop at him.

Careful planning, proper timing—I picked the spot where the trail
and the brush were just right. I stopped Smut, and when the mustang's

head came up to see what was happening, I flipped the loop onto his neck. The yearling didn't even realize he was caught. I pulled the rope up ever so gently to tighten the loop and let the youngster follow me on to camp.

The yearling was the only one we got that day. The Phantom and his bunch went ten different directions when they came to the pass and Gilbert tried to turn them toward the ranch. Some went to the mountain, some went through the pass, and one came back to me.

That yearling grew to be a fine animal. I broke him and named him Frosty. He was a joy to ride, quick to learn, and pretty as a picture. Sometimes I look at him and think he might have had noble ancestors—maybe Arabian.

We moved back to the Johnson Ranch Thursday night and I was sure the dance would be held without me, but late that night as I was preparing my damp bed for another tussle, Sid said to me, "They need the buckboard back at the H-D Ranch. Would you take it up there tomorrow? Then meet me back at the Thomas horse camp Monday. I'll bring your saddle horses."

"Sure, I can do that," I said.

I don't know if they really needed the buckboard. No one asked about it or used it while I was at the H-D. But I got to the dance and I really believe that is what Sid wanted me to do. Maybe a romantic feeling had come into his generous heart.

The Sevina

Sevina is the color of a horse. Some people might call it a roan and others could refer to it as a pinto; but horses that have much more white hair than sorrel on their coat and have a sorrel or mottled mane and tail, I call sevina. Most of them have bally faces and generally some of their legs are also white. There was such a horse on the south end of Delno Mountain, a filly about two years old.

I received a short letter from Dad. His letters were always short and written of necessity, this one asking me to bring his gray saddle horse, Del, to the H-D Ranch. He wrote that he had traded Del for a thoroughbred stallion and that the new owner could come as far as the H-D to pick up the saddle horse.

This was almost bad news to me. Del was an excellent saddle horse, six years old, gentle to ride, and could run faster than average. I planned to use him while gathering our horses. I had others to ride but it's always hard to give up a good, gentle saddle horse. Nevertheless, I prepared to take Del the next morning. I talked my cousin, Bud, into going with me by hinting we might get a chance to catch a mustang, as our journey would take us across Delno Mountain both going to and returning from the H-D Ranch. Bud was an excitable young chap, always eager for a new adventure.

We left early, expecting to stay the first night at the Eccles Ranch, about forty miles as the crow flies from our home at Grouse Creek. Bud was riding his sorrel horse, Rock, a lively, easy-traveling gelding. I rode Del and led my palomino, a mustang that had lived on the south end of Delno until my father roped him when he was three years old. I thought I'd save the palomino for the ride home and the possible race we hoped to generate with some wild horses. It was the last of August and the weather was warm so we traveled light, a couple sandwiches tied in a light jacket behind the saddle and enough oats for two feedings for our horses. The oats were sort of an emergency measure in case we were detained and had to lay out a night.

We traveled along at an easy trot, sitting flat in our saddles and talking of our possibilities, when we found some mustangs. Bud told me of a sevina filly that ranged from Grassy Mountain to the south of Delno. Two government trappers he knew told the story to him. The filly was supposed to be beautiful to look at and could run like the wind. Of course we knew that all wild horses are beautiful to look at when they are on a mountainside with their heads in the air and the breeze blowing their manes and tails. That little distance between them and you covers all the blemishes and tends to make the young look older and the old look younger, thus you see the ideal horse. When a horse cuts away in a cloud of dust it is hard to judge how fast it is running, but you imagine it must be very fast because it is soon out of sight, leaving only an image and a trail of dust. We couldn't be sure if the sevina was young and beautiful or if she was small and old, but we hoped for a chance to find out.

As we crossed the Death Valley basin, Bud showed me the cave where his brother found an old pistol. There were human bones in the cave, and we thought a wounded man might have hidden in the cave and died there, and that the pistol had been his. None of the old-timers could recall such an incident, and it remained a mystery as to who it might be. A search for gold or coin on the cave floor revealed nothing, so if the person was a bank robber he must have hidden his loot elsewhere.

We watered our horses and ate our lunch at Chicken Springs, and then followed the road out on top and rode down a long ridge to the Mill Creek corral. Several thousand sheep had been sheared there over the past few years, and the area close around was practically denuded by overgrazing. Just south of the mouth of Mill Creek were the remains of an old blacksmith shop—a few posts still standing from the framework and a short, thick cedar stump scarred by hammer and hot irons, indicating it had been used as a base for an anvil. That was all that was left of the lost silver mine.

Supposedly two brothers had come to the area years before, found a silver mine, and worked it two years. There was trouble in their family back east so they went home to help, taking what they could with them and burying the rest, including the mine. They never returned and the silver mine remained lost.

We rode out of the bottom of Granite Creek, the main creek that flowed down to Thousand Springs Creek below Crittenden Ranch, went west up a steep draw and then crossed a flat bench and climbed to the top of Delno above the Mitchell mine near Round Top. From here we could see a panorama of low mountain ranges, the home of many wild horses.

Directly below us was a bunch of seven, led by a nice buckskin stud that was eight or ten years old. His mane and tail were long and tangled, the tail almost touching the ground. The horses immediately gathered when they saw us, and then followed a black mare as she ran around the side of the mountain to the south.

We followed them, not trying to catch up, all the way to the south slope. We guessed the buckskin stud and his bunch were the horses running down Division Canyon, their dust hanging close to the ground all the way from the pass just below us. Three young-looking horses we thought were studs ran around each other a couple of times and followed the trail of the first bunch down the canyon.

"Too bad we couldn't take a cut at those three," I told Bud.

"Yes, that could have been interesting, but they're long gone now." Bud shifted a little in his saddle and added, "Look over there on the south ridge of Division. I can see three more bunches stirring around wondering where we are and what the excitement is that caused the buckskin stud to leave the country."

"Well, let's not keep them waiting," I said. "We have to leave the canyon this side of the flat where you can see the white horse in that bunch. Heavy trails lead west from the canyon to the low pass between those two cedar-covered knolls."

"Yes, I see them. That's near where you fellows built the trap corral, isn't it?"

"Right. The corral is in the draw north of the trails, right in the edge of the cedars where the draw narrows. Have you ever been there?"

"One time, but I didn't use the corral."

"Just as well," I said. "It's not too good. We made the fence into a wall by weaving cedar branches into the net wire. It would have been much better if it was open so the horses could see through. Much better. Remember that when you build a trap corral, Bud."

"I hope I never build one. It's more fun to run at a bunch of them mustangs and rope whichever one gets in your way."

"Let's move a little and see how many bunches start running. We have two on the run now if we count the three young studs as a bunch." I kicked Del gently with my spurs and started down toward Division Canyon. It was about a mile from where we were to the edge of the cedar line on the long south ridge of the canyon. We jogged along the horse trails across the face of the mountain. By the time we got to the trees we could see dust from seven bands of wild horses, all running south toward Thousand Springs Creek. The white horse and the others with it didn't move from the flat where they were feeding. We went down the ridge as far as the trails across the canyon and then turned west toward the Eccles Ranch.

"These horses are sure wild," Bud commented. "They all run at the same time whether you chase them or not. How are we going to get close enough to put a rope on one?"

"When we come back we won't ride out on the face of the mountain and start a bunch running like we did today. I won't be leading a horse, either, and that will make a difference. If we stay out of sight in the cedars and plan ahead a little, I think we can get close to something. We might not get the sevina you dream about, but maybe we can get into the roan pacer's bunch. He has about eleven or twelve. A young stud from his bunch would be nice to ride. Did you see anything at all that could be called a sevina?"

"No, I sure didn't. Two buckskins in the first bunch and a gray, a sorrel, and a bay below them. The other bunches were all dark colors except the white one."

"The white one is a stud that's been around for some time. A fellow roped him one day and broke his rope. That was four years ago and he was a full-aged horse then. He must be twelve years old by now."

"We don't even want him then," Bud said. "He'd be a rough one to break at that age."

The conversation broke and we rode to the Eccles Ranch, stayed all night, and then went to the H-D Ranch the next day, a twenty-mile ride. We left Del with the ranch foreman, telling him how gentle the horse was so he wouldn't be afraid to ride him for the new owner when he came. The following day we went back to the Eccles Ranch, and bright and early on the fourth day from home we started back across the south end of Delno, filled with anticipation at the prospect of catching one of those elusive wild mustangs. The sevina would be our choice, but we would first have to find her, if there really was such an animal.

We ate breakfast at six o'clock and were in Division Canyon before ten. We saw the white stud and his bunch near where they were two days before. The roan pacer and bunch were two ridges east of them, but they saw us before we saw them and they disappeared among the cedars.

We rode carefully from pass to ridge to draw, and though we saw several bunches of horses, there was no sevina, and our luck was all bad.

Not once did we get close enough to have any chance of running into a bunch to use our ropes. By early afternoon we were quite disappointed. Most of the wild horse country was behind us.

"Let's ride over toward Grassy Mountain and lay out tonight," Bud suggested. "We have oats for the horses and the bunchgrass must be plentiful; all of the mustangs are fat. It's early enough for our horses to get a good feed if we let them graze until dark. I know they haven't had any water but they'll make it 'til noon. We could have a chance at some mustangs as they come out from Crittenden Spring in the morning, and then ride on in and water our horses."

Before I could answer, Bud held up his hand. He was a little in front of me and I stopped beside him. Even before he pointed I could see horses all over the side of little Grassy Mountain, a smooth knoll to the west of the main mountain. I counted nine, but the rest of the bunch went around the knoll to the north before I got a chance to count them. What excited me most was the lead one of the nine: it was a light color, maybe a palomino or a sevina.

We looked at each other for a couple of minutes without speaking. When we looked back the horses were all out of sight. Each of us dismounted and reset our saddles in preparation for the chase. My palomino was most anxious as this was home to him; four years ago he was running wild in this area. The sevina might even be his half sister. If she was, she would be worth catching; my palomino was a good one.

Bud spoke eagerly, "Let me go around the south side of the knoll and meet them head on. I think my horse is fast enough to run in the middle of the bunch to the draw here in front of us and I'll have one caught by then. You pick your place wherever you want. They're sure to come on these trails right where we're sitting, or if the bunch is close together they might go above the trees. What do you think?"

"All right, you meet them and don't worry about me. If they come this way I'll get into them. If that's the sevina and you miss her I'll get her for sure." I knew my "for sure" was just boasting. When you chase wild horses nothing is certain until after a catch is made.

Bud went around the knoll, and when I saw him again there were horses all around him—in front, behind, and on both sides. They were running and he was swinging his loop looking for a good catch—anything young, least of all an old mare.

I loosed the reins on my horse, Pal, and he galloped right into the middle of that dusty mess. There must have been more than twenty head, counting colts and all. I watched the dark ones go by, one after the other, wanting so much a chance at the sevina. I saw Bud through the dust with one on his rope. It looked like a young horse, not full grown.

From back of Bud came the sevina, white mane and tail flying in the air. I judged my distance to her and to the bottom of the draw filled with high sagebrush. We would all come together at the same time. I knew I had to make my throw just before we entered the brush and put a couple of quick dallies around the horn. I didn't want to lose my rope in the high brush.

I started to swing my rope and Pal sensed the situation, lunging recklessly through the shorter sage toward the filly. Once—twice—three times I made that seagrass rope sing around my head and then with all the strength I could muster, I threw the loop at that pretty yellow head. It circled her neck one jump before she entered the heavy brush and I flipped the noose tight and dallied with one smooth motion. I knew ahead of time this is what I would have to do and it worked to perfection.

Pal followed the sevina filly through the tall sagebrush to the open hillside beyond where I pulled him up and examined my prize. She was a beauty. Her teeth showed she was two years old the past spring. She was quite tall and rangy, with a bally face, four white legs, and a nearly white mane and tail.

Bud caught a light bay, three-year-old stud. He said he couldn't get to the sevina because too many horses were in the way. There we were, two happy men—and just when we were about to give up. Just give us one more chance, we had thought. And here it was laid right in our laps—all we could ever hope for.

The Butterfly Stud

I was sitting there on a big rock at the edge of a serviceberry patch watching a bunch of wild horses coming in to water. My big gray horse named Dusty was tied back of me among some taller bushes to shield him from sight. I wanted the wild horses to drink their fill before I startled them. In fact, if the black stud we named Butterfly wasn't there I didn't want the wild horses at all.

We were between jobs after shipping fifteen carloads of beef the day before. The boss said we'd take a day to relax, and the whole cow outfit of eleven riders plus the cook and nighthawk were out there on the mountain to capture the Butterfly stud.

I was sent to find the stud and his bunch and take them the first heat of what was to be a daylong relay, if necessary. Riders were posted at intervals along the intended route, the object being to run the stud and his bunch into the cavy of about a hundred sixty horses being held on Red Point Mountain. There they could graze until the wild horses came. At that time all the horses would be taken across the railroad tracks to Loomis.

We thought if we could get the Butterfly stud to cross the tracks, it would be a big step in our favor. The stud was fast, built like a thoroughbred race horse, and wilder than anything I had ever seen. He would quit a bunch for no reason at all and take off on his own. If he was on Knoll Mountain when we started him he would run to Red Point, and if he was on Red Point he would run to Knoll Mountain. The distance as the crow flies is about fifteen miles, but with pressure the stud could be made to run down Burnt Creek Canyon to the road where he always turned south, making a wide circle back to Red Point. That would add twenty miles to the course.

We had run at Butterfly more than a dozen times. Single rider or in bunches it was always the same—when pressed too hard the stud quit the bunch and outran any horse we happened to be riding. With some luck, today would be different.

The horses were coming to water at the cold spring high on the north end of Knoll Mountain, the spring that flows down into the head of Burnt Creek from the south. I remembered how sweet and cool the water was and wished for a drink of it myself; I knew it would be a long, dry day. My next chance to drink would be noon, if I was lucky, when I reached Thousand Springs Creek at the north base of Red Point.

The lead horses walked unhesitatingly into the spring while those behind trotted hurriedly to catch up, anticipating the freshness of the clear water. I was sure it was the right bunch even before the stud, who was sort of hanging back as a lookout for trouble, finally came in sight. He was a beautiful animal, trim and refined in every way. His body glistened in the early morning sunlight, not coal black but slate black, with no white markings at all. There were fourteen horses with him—an assortment of mares with colts and others that were small and looked to be young stock.

Now that I was certain the bunch was the one I wanted, I went back through the bushes to Dusty and mounted. Keeping out of sight from the mustangs I rode down the ridge about fifty yards and then turned back toward the mountain. This was a predetermined sign to a rider now sitting on his horse on a bare knoll some distance to the south of me. He would watch and be in place to make the second run. When he rode out of sight and reappeared I knew he caught my signal.

Judging from the trails the horses used to come in to water, they had been feeding at the head of Burnt Creek and in country north toward Bell Canyon. When the mustangs started out on the trails south, feeding as they went, it pleased me considerably. My job would be much easier, for I could wait a few minutes until they fed into a sharp draw to the south and be right in the middle of them before they came out the other side. The probable course they would take would be down the open ridge south of the draw, and that led right to the second rider.

I felt a little sorry for myself. I wanted so badly to have a chance to rope the Butterfly stud, and with me being the one to start the horses, my chance of getting close enough to catch anything was indeed remote. Most of the other cowboys were better around cows. Some had never run wild horses, so the four of us who knew something of the sport drew lots to see which position we would take along the trail. I drew the starting slot and figured to give them a good run and then cut for camp.

I was mounted and ready when the wary stud left his vigil on the north rim of the draw and went out of sight. That was what I had been waiting for. I urged Dusty into a fast trot to gain the edge of the draw before I was seen. The good grass scattered through the brush in the swale kept the horses occupied, and I was galloping right at them before I was discovered.

The stud hesitated a moment to see what was challenging him, and then whirled away in the center of the band. We all hit the crest of the long ridge together. Some of the mustangs were behind me, Dusty running with them as though one of the bunch.

I took my rope down and shook out a loop. Maybe I could rope a young animal near the tail end of the bunch. No chance at the stud because he was fifty yards ahead of me and going away. Then I thought how it might look if the mustangs didn't get to the second rider where he could handle them and I came in with a yearling or an old mare. The rest of the boys would know that I had not played with the team, that I had gone solo and lost them the chance of capturing the elusive stallion. I eased Dusty up a little and let the horses pass. It would have been so easy to catch one of them, especially the young black stud that looked to be about two years old. Oh well, maybe another time.

Dusty and I ran right behind the mustangs, whooping and hollering to keep them running scared for a little over a mile, at which point I could see they were going dead center for the second rider. I eased Dusty up and let them go.

After pulling my saddle for several minutes and walking my horse around while he cooled off, I saddled again and turned toward Red Point, the goal for the horses once they made a wide circle on the flat. I jogged Dusty along on the better trails and let him walk the rough places and brush. We were almost to the top of Knoll Mountain, a long, low-ridge mountain, when I saw the mustangs below me on the flat. Apparently the fourth rider had been in a hurry to take over and turned the horses back.

I searched the country with my eyes and finally located the second rider crossing the sagebrush flat from a grove of cedars far below me. I thought if he knew where the mustangs were he could maybe give them another heat and turn them back toward the cavy on Red Point. As if reading my thought, he turned from his course toward the horses and a few minutes later had the mustangs running a second circle on the flat.

I let Dusty climb the remaining distance to the crest of Knoll Mountain and turned him left along the trails south. If there was any possible chance for me to be in a position where I could ride into the bunch again, I wanted to be ready. This second tour of the big flat would take some time. That would allow me to get to the cavy, or at least near to it.

Just before leaving the south point of the mountain, I scanned the country below me again. All three riders were with the mustangs and the horses had slowed, breaking from a trot to a slow gallop depending on the terrain. The riders were playing the mustangs quite loose, and though the stud was about a quarter mile out in front, I figured he would stay with the bunch as long as they went toward his goal of Red Point.

The cavy was spread wide across the northeast side of the smooth face of Red Point, well above the high sage at the base of the red jut of clay from which the mountain got its name. I could see the saddle horses clearly from where I was, and I turned Dusty toward them. We jogged down a gravel ridge that was bare except for an uneven growth of mountain sage and white sage; both were short and Dusty traveled easily.

It took an hour or more to follow the long ridge to the bottom and to climb the quarter mile up Red Point to the cavy. I rode directly up to Ed Murphy, who was anxiously awaiting the arrival of the mustangs.

"Did you find the stud?" he asked.

"I sure did, Ed. He and his bunch were just coming in to water at the Knoll Mountain spring. There's fifteen of them counting the Butterfly." Ed flashed a big smile before continuing.

"Are they coming this way? Did you get them started right? Where are they now?"

"The boys have all of them headed this way. I could see them from the top of Knoll. The stud was way out in the lead, but I expect he'll stay with the bunch as long as they're coming this way. When he gets into the cavy I don't know what'll happen. About half of our horses are mustangs, and some aren't very gentle. We might have our hands full trying to hold all this mess." I dismounted and pulled my gear from Dusty. He was a little tired but would make it to camp. There were a half dozen men on fresh horses that could do the running if necessary.

From above the cavy on top of a small denuded knoll, the nighthawk waved his hat and called out. The slight breeze was right and I could hear parts of what he had to say.

"They're comin'!" he called, "Along the fifty-four!" He pointed toward the east where there was a field called the fifty-four.

I quickly divined that the mustangs would cross the highway south of Whaley's station and follow the heavy horse trails from Thousand Springs Creek up the ridge south of the cavy. I soon saw I was not alone in that thinking when Sid and John started riding south toward the ridge so they could turn the wild horses into the cavy of saddle horses. While I was at it, I did some more guessing: Butterfly had never stayed in a bunch of gentle horses more than a few minutes. Why should he be different today? He was tired for sure but he was also wild, afraid of men. How could he know we wouldn't kill him? We had no way of communicating friendship to him until after he was caught and we got our hands on him. No wonder he did his best to get away. Under the same circumstances I would also.

When the stud left the bunch, as I was sure he would, where would he run? My eyes searched the area around me, studying the mountainside for the best possible route he might go. I thought he might take the most direct path back toward Knoll Mountain, the next ridge over from where I was sitting. Ed Murphy was over there, having nervously ridden in that direction when we were given the signal that the horses were coming. I walked my horse over toward him, taking my rope down as I went.

"What are you going to catch out here on the mountainside?" Ed asked quizzically.

"Probably not anything, Ed. I use my rope to keep the horses in line. If they think I might rope them they turn easier, and old Dusty is tired."

"Ya, I guess they would," Ed conceded.

"Why don't you trade places with me, Ed? Your horse is fresh and when we move out you could take the point. About all I can do is follow along." Ed turned and rode slowly back north across the small swale to the other ridge.

I tied the end of my forty-foot rope around the fork of my saddle and put a double hitch on the horn. Dusty was tired and I was not sure that I'd have time to dally if I did catch the stud. He might go by me quite fast, for he would be running downhill while I would be crossing over or skirting the mountain. The timing had to be just right to get me close enough to catch him. There would be only the interception point and then he would be gone.

When I saw Sid and John turn the mustangs and head them for the cavy, I was ready. The wild horses, though tired, were nervous. The stud was gingerly challenged by several of the saddle geldings who, themselves, had been monarchs of mares in previous years. I watched him closely as he went around among the horses, sometimes squealing defiantly or striking the ground with a forepaw. Mostly, I noticed his eyes were on the several riders who were all mounted up and anxious to move out. The stud stopped near the center of the bunch, raised his head high, and looked at each rider in turn. He emitted a low whistle. After standing a few minutes he trotted toward Sid and John, who had their ropes ready to catch him if the opportunity came, and then trotted back through the horses. I remembered what Dad had told me a few years before. "He's coming out, son. He'll go to the far side and then come out the most direct way to his range. Nothing but a rope will stop him." He was coming out, and my way too.

In my mind time stood still, and I saw every detail of what happened in the next few seconds. I saw the stud charge from the top of the bunch, gathering speed as he came, pushing and bumping horses aside until he was clear of the herd. He had twice the distance to travel, as did I, to our meeting place, but he was moving and running downgrade. Dusty responded almost feebly, so I cut him across the rump with my loop to move him faster. The stud was coming too fast—it would be a long throw. Sid and John were galloping toward me to help, but they would be too late. I swung my rope twice around my head, making a wide circle to get the full leverage of my arm, then threw as hard as I could and watched the loop sail out over the long space between us. Too far?—no! The loop hung in the air—got smaller and smaller. Finally, when it was just barely large enough to allow the stud's head to enter, the loop settled over his head and immediately cinched tight around his neck. I turned Dusty downgrade and threw my body weight into the left stirrup just in time to partially counteract the weight of the stallion as he hit the end of the rope.

Dusty stumbled and almost fell, the shock jerking horse and saddle from under me. I still stood in the left stirrup and had hold of the reins and rope, but I was standing on the ground beside Dusty. The stud fell flat on his side from the sudden jerk of the rope, and before he could get back to his feet Sid had a second rope on him. I untied mine from my saddle and handed it to John. He and Sid were both on fresh horses and could handle the stud easier than I could on my tired horse.

As Ed Murphy rode up he exclaimed, "You played a trick on me, kid!" Everyone younger than Ed was a kid to him.

"What do you mean, played a trick on you?" I countered, knowing full well that I had planned to be right there when the stud came out of the bunch.

"I was right where the stud came out until you traded me."

"Quit kiddin', Murph. You wouldn't have roped him on this mountainside."

Ed expelled a long sigh, "You're right. I was kiddin'. I wouldn't rope a gentle horse on a steep slope like that. You're nuts, kid, but that was sure a purty loop. Clear to the end of your rope."

The whole bunch of mustangs stayed with the saddle horses and we corralled them at Loomis. There were one three-year-old stud, two studs that were two years old, four mares with colts, and three fillies.

Butterfly was seven years old, and even when he was an old gentle horse he still became startled occasionally by a rider a short distance away. Memories of those many races with men on horseback must have haunted him the rest of his life.

Chalk Eye

I was riding with the Wine Cup cow outfit and we were four days from the Loomis summer range trailing nine hundred two-year-old steers, give or take a few. We were taking them to the Gallaher pasture to finish them out before shipping. Last week we had shipped thirty-six carloads cut from the top end of our herd out of Red Point. The nine hundred left were the scrubs of the herd and could do with a few more weeks of fattening.

We trailed the cattle from early morning until about noon, letting them rest through the heat of the day to keep as much flesh on them as possible. Breakfast was at two A.M. each day, and by four we were on the trail. Working this way it didn't take long to stay in the sack all night.

This particular morning I had left the herd below Texas Springs and was headed back to Loomis, where Rex and I were breaking saddle horses. Two months earlier we had started with sixty-two head and were down to the last twelve when I went to help with the drive. Working alone, Rex could only ride the horses we had already started breaking. He needed my help to tie the rest up and break them to lead.

I was riding Rowdy, a bay standard-bred horse that lived up to his name. He could travel slow if you coaxed him, but he would rather trot or gallop and could run as fast as any of my horses. The reason I was on him this day was because he came to the edge of the horses in the rope corral just as I was approaching with my bridle. I could see his head against the starry sky with the long, white strip in his forehead and the white snip on his nose. I gently put my arm around his neck and bridled him before he became lost among the eighty or more horses of the cavy. I thought how nice it would be to have all white horses so you could see them in the dark, but if all the horses were white it would be hard to distinguish one from another.

I had ridden Rowdy the first day out of Loomis; Gray Freckles and the red roan I called Ed carried me the other days. It was Rowdy's turn again and he was fresh from the short rest. We galloped along, now and then holding to a trot or walking short distances. I wasn't paying much attention to what was going on around me—just thinking of Rex and how he might be getting by with the saddle broncs.

Rex was slight of build, but spunky. He could ride a bucker if given an even break and was careful most of the time. Taking chances when you are alone is not a smart thing to do, and I was sure Rex would be careful.

I wondered how he might make it with the tall brown we called Abe. Abe was skittish and wont to whirl away and buck when you started to get on. Maybe Rex would put a rope on Abe's front feet and drop it loose when he was in the saddle.

Then there was the roan ridge runner. Wild and defiant, afraid of everything that moved, he was certainly a challenge to ride and had been a real rough one to capture; but that's another story. I recalled how each morning as the roan topped out on the ridge above the corral he'd stop for a moment to look around and then give a loud whistle, his head high and tail curled, a beautiful picture to a horse lover. I wondered which one of the cowboys would be lucky and draw the ridge runner to add to his string. He'd be a good saddle horse someday, but he'd keep his rider awake for many days before settling down. Maybe Rex would work these two around in the corral and wait for me to get back.

That thought making me more anxious, I let Rowdy have his head to gallop for a short distance again. I was sitting flat in the saddle enjoying the easy motion of my horse when we came around a bend in the trail from behind a few cedar trees. There in front of me was a mud wallow spring someone had named Dinner Spring, and all around it, trying to water, was a band of mustangs. Rowdy pulled up short and I thought he was going to whistle, so I patted his neck gently and spoke to him softly to take his attention from the wild horses. They were so intent on getting to the water that they hadn't noticed me. I turned Rowdy around and rode back into the cedars to fix my saddle and tighten my cinches. I knew I was going to try to rope one of them, and if I was successful, Rex would just have to get along as best he could until I could get there.

Rowdy was all perked up and would hardly stand still while I reset my Hamley saddle and tightened the cinches. He was ready for the race and as soon as I shook out a loop, so was I.

My position among the trees was nearly a half mile from the spring and I watched quietly as the horses drank from the puddles along the edge of the seep hole. When the holes were dry they carefully edged out into the mud to reach the good water at the heart of the spring. As some drank their fill and backed out of the muddy ooze, others took their place. I counted twelve to fourteen head as they milled around the water hole; it was hard to tell exactly how many because of the distance and their constant movement.

One time I was sure there were cows among the horses because I could see so much white on the heads of two of the animals; however, it was not long before I determined two horses had mostly white heads, each with white along one side of its neck. When they turned the other way the white didn't show. This verified a story I had heard from a cowboy two years ago, about a brown mare with a white head and white legs and a colt with the same markings. He tried to catch the colt but his horse was too slow. He saw them high up in Bell Canyon, only a few miles from this spring. They could have grazed a little off their range and come in for water, or maybe some cowboy had chased them, though I didn't know of any that should be in the area. At any rate they were here at Dinner Spring, sinking to their knees and churning the mud around the edge of the water hole trying to get their fill.

If the cowboy's story was true, and I had no reason to doubt it, the smaller of the horses with white heads would be a two-year-old stud. He was my objective that morning. Of course circumstances might have entered into the picture to change my plans. If I couldn't get a good run at him I would take whichever one came within the range of my loop.

The white-headed mare and her two-year-old offspring were hesitant to wade out in the churned mud for their water. Most of the horses had their fill and were leaving the spring when they finally wallowed out and began drinking. Rowdy and I were moving toward them at a fast walk, almost shielded from their view by the point of a sagebrush-covered ridge. With luck we could ride up close before coming out into the open flat, where they surely would see us.

I was keyed up for the chase and Rowdy was stepping short and quick, eager to break into a gallop at my command. We came closer and closer to the spring. All the horses were gone except the two with white heads, who had their rumps toward me and were craning their necks to reach the water without walking deeper into the quagmire. The horses trailing from the water saw us and stopped. One of them whinnied a message to the two at the water hole. They raised their heads but were hesitant to leave before they had their fill, and they still didn't see me approaching from behind.

It was not until the bunch of wild horses started to run that they realized there was danger, and by then it was too late. By the time they struggled out of the mud I was close upon them, and when they started up the slope toward Knoll Mountain, I passed the mare and headed for the stud. It really wasn't a very good race. The young stud was full of water and Rowdy had galloped enough to be warmed up and ready. In less than a half mile I tossed my rope on the stud and pulled him to a stop.

The young horse was so full of water that the short gallop made him sick and unable to run further. I know I would be sick trying to run with my stomach so full of water, and I expect it would be no different for him. I thought of hobbling the stud and trying for the mare who had turned to the side and was walking slowly through the cedars toward Bell Canyon. I soon changed my mind when I considered how difficult it might be to get the two of them to Loomis before dark. It was nearly forty miles, a long day without leading a horse. Leading two would be impossible.

The stud was handsome. He was a little rangy, but he would soon fill out with the better feed of ranch life. A winter or two on oats and hay and he might grow to be near a thousand pounds, a nice size for a saddle horse. The white markings on his head and neck were different from any I had seen. He was a wide bally, looking from the right side. The white ran across the left side of the face and jaw, and he was white along the neck to about halfway down. He had a moon eye or a glassy eye, as some call it. I'm glad he had a gentle nature, because it is hard to determine what a horse is about to do by looking into an expressionless moon eye. Another eye might show the fire or the calm nature of the horse, but the moon eye just reflects back at you.

After a short time I had worked myself close to the stud and got my hands on him; from then on it was easy to lure him next to Rowdy and get them moving together. We circled around through the brush awhile and then headed for the road at the mouth of Burnt Creek Canyon. I was lucky no one was traveling the road that day; we were able to move along at a good trot most of the way to Loomis, arriving just before dark.

"What kind of a chalk-eyed Hereford do you have there?" Rex blurted, meeting me at the gate. He could see me coming as I rode down the hill above the corral, kicking loose rocks and gravel.

"Isn't he a beauty, Rex?" I said laughingly. "He'll be a real show horse."

"Where did you catch him? Is he the one from Bell Canyon, the one Murphy saw a couple years ago?"

"He's the one, I suppose. I caught him just off the Dinner Spring water hole. He couldn't outrun Rowdy with his tummy full of water."

"Well, I don't suppose he could, and maybe not any other time either. That Rowdy steps right along. I'll trade you Chipmunk for him. I need a horse like Rowdy in case I want to catch an antelope someday."

"No, Rex, I better keep Rowdy. You wouldn't like him. He's too nervous."

"All right, but when we're working cows, you just remember I tried to trade Chipmunk for Rowdy and you refused."

Rex named the stud Chalk Eye and we kept him around with the saddle broncs the rest of the summer. Although he was only two years old, we each rode him a few times, keeping close to the corral so we wouldn't ride him too hard.

Chalk Eye was very gentle. He grew up as a pet with the cavy and then made his way into a saddle string at four years old. He never displayed fear of a man on horseback like so many mustangs do. Though not very fast, he became a good, useful cow horse.

Sid Paskett on Snowshoe, Loomis, 1934. Note bedroll, used also to carry gear.

Grey Eagle, saddled up and ready to ride.

Parley Paskett at Squaw Creek, 1939.

Peoho, the desert mustang who broke his leg, Squaw Creek, 1937.

Goldie, ready to catch Grey Eagle.

The palomino mustang captured on Delno Mountain, 1932.

A mustang colt, Loomis, 1939.

Sid Paskett, Rex Hill, Parley Paskett, Ben Jurjens, Roy Johnson, and Howard Whitehouse at Desert Well #1, 1938.

The buckskin stud from the desert.

Sturdy, high fences needed to confine wild mustangs, Thomas horse camp, 1937.

Parley Paskett with the six-year-old stud, Possum, Squaw Creek, 1937.

Parley Paskett with the sevina filly, 1933.

Parley J. Paskett on Slippers, Montello Desert, 1938.

Branding a wild stud, Thurston horse camp, 1937.

A Tail in the Dark

Three of us, Gilbert, Sid, and myself, stayed all night at the Utah Construction Company's Shafter #1 Well located a few miles from Shafter, Nevada, on the Western Pacific Railroad. Gilbert was foreman of the Johnson Ranch, about twenty miles northwest of Shafter, and Sid came down from the Gamble Ranch, fifty miles north on Thousand Springs Creek. He brought groceries and was on his way to the Shafter #2 Well, twenty miles south near a promontory called Black Point.

It was March 18, and the chill of early spring felt cool on my face although the sun was shining in a mostly clear sky. Sid and Gilbert went on ahead in the car and I was to ride my horse and meet them about halfway to Black Point.

"We'll see if we can start a bunch of mustangs up the flat. If we can, we'll give them a good run in the car and you can take them from us and run them on toward the Johnson Ranch. We'll ride the car to the ranch, saddle our horses, and come out to meet you." Sid's voice was matter-of-fact. If they could get some wild horses started in the right direction, he was certain the plan would work.

Gilbert, the more quiet of the two, was soft spoken with his advice. "Keep them running but don't press them too hard or they will split up and go several directions. They're afraid of you only at a distance. When you get close they can see what you are and they're not afraid to challenge you. You know how to do it. Play them all the way, but keep them running."

I respected Gilbert's advice because I knew he had captured several mustangs off the desert by making much the same run as I would that day. I remembered Gilbert patting my rope as he walked by my horse just before we started our trip that morning. "Don't get in a big hurry to use your rope. You know if you catch one, that's all you'll have, and the rest of the bunch will go free." Then he questioned, "Do you want me to take your rope in the car? Might keep you from getting too anxious to toss it on one."

"No, Gilbert," I replied. "Remember the day we bought those five wild ones out of the Collar and Elbow? We had them run to a nub, but they wouldn't cross the Shafter Short Line Railroad. I really wished for my rope then, and I think I'll carry it with me from now on."

Gilbert slammed the car door and they were off, leaving me to jog along quietly by myself. I was riding a tall bay horse called Dean. Sired by a thoroughbred stallion, he was one of only two horses I ever rode that could chase a mustang until it dropped from exhaustion. I wanted so much for them to start a band of eight or ten mustangs so I could try my luck at taking them all the way to the ranch.

I pushed Dean as fast as he would walk, and often he would break into a slow jog. It's a joy to ride a horse that can walk fast. I like the rhythm of the hoofbeat, the easy flow of the body as we progress, man and horse moving together as one unit. If a horse is not a good walker, I crowd him until he develops an easy stride. Every horse can be improved given proper encouragement.

Looking to my right toward Johnson Mountain, I could see a few flaky fog clouds barely covering the mountaintop. South and beyond Little Lake Pass, Spruce Mountain also harbored a few white clouds, and forty miles to the south, directly ahead of me, a thunderhead hung over Dolly Varden Peak. The rest of the sky, save two small spots of sheep clouds, was clear.

I passed the gravel butte at the head of Steptoe Valley and could see several bands, some already moving toward the Ryegrass Patch water hole. If mustangs are continually chased or worried, they generally water in the late evening or early morning; some water during the dead of night, especially if the moon is bright. These horses, however, watered about every two or three days. They came in to drink and left of their own volition. Few horsemen ever challenged them to a race.

The Ryegrass Patch, a watering place covering several acres, was named thus because of the several bunches of ryegrass located on its west fringe. The water gathers on a low hardpan area to about two feet deep, remaining until it evaporates or is used up by the horses. There were several bunches near the water, all appearing as small dots; but even at that distance (about five miles maximum), I could tell they were of different colors.

To my left the Toana range stretched like a guardian from Silver Zone to White Horse Pass. It was covered with scrub cedar and piñon pine, the winter snow still blanketing its crest and side nearly down to the desert floor. The ground was soft under Dean's shod hooves and I could hear their clop only when I crossed the many hardpan spots.

I figured the snow would keep the mustangs from the mountain, thus alleviating the problem of riding both sides of the bunch. The car could follow behind long enough to get the bunch past the Shafter #1 Well, while I rode the west side and kept them from the water. I mulled over several things that might happen, considering what I would do or could do and remembering there is no set pattern; each horse reacts differently. To know exactly what to do ahead of time was impossible. Yet I thought. I recalled instances and picked trails, noting the small washes, the thicker brush, and the smooth desert as well as the rough. I knew that a little planning could keep my horse from some rough running and save his strength and precious wind. It would take all Dean's strength to follow those mustangs the forty or more miles from the desert to Silver Zone Pass and across the valley west to the Johnson Ranch.

I looked again at the mountains around me. The small fog clouds on Johnson Mountain were gone and most of the white cap had disappeared from Spruce, but the thunderhead that hung so tenaciously to Dolly Varden was growing rapidly in size and density. That was fine, as long as it stayed down there. I certainly didn't want it to drift north and soak me and the ground I wanted to race over.

I noticed a bunch of mustangs about a mile west of me. There were eight palominos in this bunch, and grays, roans, and bays in other bands nearby. How nice it would be to just ride among them and pick the one I might desire. It would be a hard choice because of the many beautiful animals.

It was near noon when I spotted something in front of me that I thought could be the car chasing a bunch of horses. Black Point appeared as a mirage, lifted by heat waves, floating above the desert floor.

I stopped Dean and dismounted. If I was to reset my saddle and relax for a few minutes, now would be the only time. After I started with the horses there would be little time for hesitation until the horses were in the field at the ranch.

The day was not warm enough for a mirage in any direction except to the south toward Black Point. The horses were much closer then, and I determined that the car was following the old, worn out trail road and the mustangs were about a hundred yards above the road nearer to the

Toana range. I tried to count the horses as they ran, single file, across a low ridge, but I couldn't get a good count until they were almost even with me. The gentle swales and ridges were not as easy to run on as the marked trail road the car was following.

Dean had his ears pricked up and was eager to go, but I held him until I was quite certain the horses were far enough beyond me that they would not turn back. The lead mare was a light bay with a black mane and tail and a small white star on her forehead. She was a racy-looking animal, a little larger than any horse in the bunch except the stallion. He was bay also, light enough to be almost buckskin in color with black points, a black mane and tail, and dark stockings about to his knees and hocks. He was running easily, stopping now and then to see if he was still being followed, and then quickly overtook the others with long, loping strides.

I mounted Dean and galloped into position alongside the horses. My presence stirred the mustangs to increase their speed for about a half mile and then they eased up a little into a gallop that they could probably hold for hours. It was going to be a long way to the ranch.

Dean threw up his head and looked toward the mountain. As I turned my head to follow his gaze, I could see a fresh bunch of mustangs come out from a small grove of cedar trees, approaching at an angle that would intercept our horses. I didn't like the situation, but there was nothing I could do.

The two bunches came close together and the studs met in a galloping challenge for a few moments. They squealed and kicked and mostly just threatened each other. Then the new stud, a slim, dark brown with no white at all on him, hurried to catch his own bunch led by a sorrel bally mare. They took the lead and stayed about a quarter mile out front.

The bunch that had already galloped several miles was comprised of bay horses, while the horses in the other bunch were sorrel with bally faces except for their monarch, a dark brown stud. I guessed that the sorrels had been ruled by a sorrel bally stud and that the brown, whipping him out because of age or injury, had taken his harem.

Once, I tried to let the lead bunch cross in front of me but they were too close to the others to make a clean break, so I hurried up alongside and held all of them high above the road until they hit the trail for Silver Zone Pass. Many of the horses spent the summer months in and around Silver Zone, so it was not too hard to guide them in that direction. Maybe this was where they would have gone on their own accord, but I like to think that I put them there.

The car kept going on the road toward the well, carrying my hope of success with it. I needed Sid and Gilbert and fresh horses to put the mustangs in the field when I arrived. I glanced at the sun and divined it would be near dark, if I got them to the field at all. First I would have to outrun them on the east side to turn them from the pass toward the Johnson Ranch. I also had to get them across the railroad track, which might not be too rough; they had probably crossed it many times on their own while grazing or traveling to and from the summer range.

Dean was galloping easily, and I could feel the power of his reserve strength. We crossed behind the wild horses and skirted a ridge, placing us high enough above them to have a downhill run when I would attempt to turn the two bunches, keeping them from going through Silver Zone Pass. I would have to contend with a highway, railroad tracks, and several deep cuts they would go through, so I wanted a smooth ridge and downgrade in my favor.

As we crested the ridge I could see that I was just barely in time— just enough time to let Dean walk a few steps and get his breath before the race. I caught the horses unaware. They knew we had dropped behind, but they were surprised when Dean and I showed up on top of the ridge, halfway up alongside of them.

The bay stud passed his mares one by one and was in the lead, closing in on the brown stud when the brown started passing his mares. The two monarchs were straining hard to outdistance us, but they were barely keeping even. Dean still had a reserve of speed I could call on if needed. In just a short distance the studs and Dean had outrun the mares and were matching stride for stride, hurtling headlong toward a large cut that swallowed the Western Pacific Railroad.

Time hung suspended and the many things that could happen flashed through my mind. My hand was resting on the strap that held my rope. Should I try to shake out a loop and catch the brown stud? He was about five to seven years old and would be a good candidate for a saddle horse. The bay stud was too old—maybe eleven to thirteen. I had only a few seconds to make up my mind. If the horses didn't turn and the stud raced me all the way to the track, I would have to catch him or come out of the race empty handed. Automatically I took the rope from the strap that held it and shook out a loop. I whirled it above my head and screamed at the studs. A few more jumps and I would have to let the brown pass in front of me and try to catch him.

The bay stud, much more tired than the brown, slackened his stride and turned along the track, heading directly toward the ranch. The next moment I saw the brown falter and turn also. My chance to catch either of them was gone and somehow I was sort of happy. I had eighteen wild horses, some of them real tired, and I wanted to put all of them in the field at the ranch.

Except for the brown stud, both bunches crossed over the tracks and headed for Maverick Pass. He stayed on the south side of the track, ran close to the track along a fill, and headed back toward the desert. I don't think the rest of the mustangs ever saw him go. The thought came to me that I could have had that brown rascal, but he was gone and I just waved at him and hurried across the tracks to keep up with the other horses.

Dean was not pulling on the bit any more after that exhausting race, but there were a lot of trot and gallop miles left in him. I pulled him from a gallop to a lively trot to give him a chance to get his wind back. The sun was setting and I had about twelve miles to go before I could hope for relief from Sid and Gilbert on fresh horses.

I noticed the bay stud had given up the lead to the old sorrel bally mare of the second bunch and was following along behind all of the horses. The extra exertion of the race had taken nearly all his strength, and he was content to be last in line.

The sun went down and the purple sage took on a more subdued gray color. The air was calm, but a fresh chill replaced the shallow warmth of the early spring sun. Riding at a trot and a gallop for many miles keeps one's blood circulating rapidly. My body was warm—almost too warm—and I welcomed the extra coolness of the evening.

It was almost dark when I saw two riderless horses standing some distance apart down in the high rabbit brush near the field. I knew it would be Sid and Gilbert hunched under their horses waiting for me to pass them by so the mustangs would not scare and scatter back across the flat to the desert.

I was glad when the horses turned at the wing fence and followed it to the gate. They all bunched there, and it was so dark that I couldn't see for sure what was holding them up. Soon they started to break through the gate and trot out into the high brush. The tight group in the gate disappeared and all that was left was the old sorrel bally, the lead mare. She came straight at us, ears back and mouth open, and vanished into the darkness of the night.

Gilbert said, "She can't go far. Wait here and I'll be back. Give me about an hour."

The hour went by and it was dark except for the stars. There was no moon at all, and the light of evening had faded from the west long ago.

I heard a noise about the same time my horse pricked up his ears. Sid's horse showed signs of excitement as well. We listened intently and could hear cursing and yelling; then all was silent again. We rode toward the noise and as we got nearer sounds of scuffling and cursing guided us until we rode right up to Gilbert. He had the sorrel mare all right, but he was at a great disadvantage: he didn't have a rope and the mare wouldn't drive anywhere. She just stood there and kicked. Gilbert had taken her long tail and wrapped the end of it around the horn of his saddle.

"I've never been so happy to see a man with a rope in all my life," Gilbert said, chuckling just a little. "You two can carry your ropes all the time if you want. I won't say another word against a rope."

We got seventeen that day, but we lost the best one—the brown stud.

Murphy

"Well, he got away again," Ed Murphy said to me as he rode up where I was unsaddling my horse. Ed was a stocky, square-shouldered man of about fifty. His hair was showing gray under the edge of his battered Stetson, and he moved slowly like a man who had spent years in the saddle.

"Who got away again, Murphy? You been chasing mustangs this morning instead of rounding up those gentle mares?" I was kidding him a little. He was a good, dependable rider and didn't go chasing if he had other things to accomplish.

"Ya, I get off on a faint trail once in a while. Especially when I see that blue-gray stud over in Dead Man. He sure is a beaut—blue-gray color and dapple marks so even they could have been traced from a silver dollar. Today he saw me first and Little Wildcat wasn't fast enough to even put me close." Little Wildcat was a mustang gelding Ed was riding—a good horse but a better cow horse than mustanger.

"If I'd been on Piute instead of Wildcat the story would be different," Ed continued. "Piute's big, but he sure can gallop. Those long legs of his carry him through the brush like he's travelin' on air. If I go out there again tomorrow I'm gonna ride Piute and see if the gray can outrun *him*."

"Where'd the stud go, Murph? Did he head down the long ridge south of Dead Man like he generally does, or was he going back toward Black Mountain?" I had seen the stud three days before at the head of Willow Creek south of Black Mountain. By being careful I got away without starting the bunch. My horse was tired that day and, hoping for a better chance at him later, I left his bunch grazing on the hillside.

"He was around the ridge north of where you saw him the other day—almost to the head of Brush Creek. I rode right into them and the race was on. We didn't have a chance right from the start. They went south across Willow Creek and the head of Dead Man, then turned east off the mountain toward the cedar ridges."

"I think they're long gone from here, Ed. Often when they run like that they follow the big cedar ridge south of Dead Man and cross Toana Flat, not even stopping 'til they reach Thomas Mountain. I've seen them at North Spring twice, so they range here and there both. You've had your last chance at them for several days."

"When I leave this fall to go back to my place in South Dakota, you ask for Piute, will ya? Try for a run at that stud sometime. I know Piute could catch him. Especially on a little upgrade." Ed went back to South Dakota about every two years to work "his place," as he called it. When his grubstake money ran out he came back to punch cows for another two years. He had returned from his place two years back when I first met him.

"All right," I said, "I'll just do that. We'll name the stud Murphy after you, and when you come back I'll have him broke so you can ride him."

We finished stripping our horses and headed for the chuck wagon. I looked across the draw at the herd of horses we had gathered the last few days—about 150, nearly all colors, shapes, and sizes. That afternoon we would brand the colts, cut the studs, and turn them back to the range, keeping the ones fit to break for saddle or work horses.

The next day I would help Rex take the saddle broncs to Loomis, and Ed Murphy would go back to the cow wagon where he'd work until the end of the month. I wouldn't see Ed again before he left, so I spoke to him as he plodded along ahead of me.

"Ed, you be careful back there in them Dakota Hills." Ed stopped, I caught up to him, and we continued side by side.

"When ya leavin', Ed?" I asked just to make conversation. I already knew when he was leaving.

"About ten days. I'll work the month out so I'll have a full check. Then I'll saddle my canary and head east." His canary was the bright yellow Model A Ford coupe that was presently under a shed at the H-D Ranch. It was also covered with an old tarp to keep the bird droppings off. Ed was proud of the canary, giving it the best of care. If you bought the gas he would haul you anywhere, but he never let anyone else drive his coupe.

Nights followed days in close succession and Murphy was soon on his way to South Dakota. His horses were turned loose with the cavy to be rested and fresh, awaiting a new cowboy. I remembered what Ed told me that day about Piute being a good horse to run mustangs. It was early fall when Rex and I put the saddle broncs we had started in the cavy to be distributed, and while the cowboys were choicing and bartering for the better broncs, I made a trade for Piute.

Ed was right. Piute was a good, big, strong horse that could run better than most. His head was as long as a wet week, and I had to splice an extension on the headstall of my bridle to accommodate him. He wore a number three shoe, too big a foot for a saddle horse. In fact, when I asked for a set of number three shoes for Piute, the storekeeper asked if I was going to shoe the chuck wagon team. I told him no, that I was putting shoes on my race horse, which brought a chuckle from everyone in earshot. There were, however, several redeeming features about the big brown Piute. The wide bally face and white socks high up his legs set him apart from other horses, and his frame, though massive, was refined. A real slim neck fastened to long, sloping shoulders could have looked good on a much smaller horse. He had a deep barrel chest I first noticed when I had to let my billet out three holes so my cinch would span his girth. His legs were clean and well muscled and his back, though long, was straight and strong. The first time I rode him I galloped out through the sage and found he was a fearless runner, jumping the tall sage as it came in his path, never dodging or breaking his long stride. I knew Piute and I would have some good times together.

When winter came we cut our saddle horses down to four per man and turned the others out on the range to rest. That was a lot different than having the seventeen head I was using during the fall roundup. I kept Piute, however, because he was tall enough to keep my feet up out of the snow and was strong on the rope in case I had work to do on the feed ground. Sometimes a weak cow would get stuck in a bog when drinking and would have to be pulled out. Piute was exceptionally good at such work.

The winter went by uneventfully. The two seven-year-old mustangs I was breaking gentled nicely and my fourth horse, a catch colt of a half-thoroughbred mare, liked to buck a little each day either in the morning or when he could find an excuse during the day. Five years old and fully alive, he calmed down considerably by the first of the year. I had to sit tight in my saddle sometimes, but I never did have to walk in. When you know you have to ride or walk, it makes you hang on a little tighter to that Hamley.

About March 20 I was asked to ride from the H-D to the Gamble to help dehorn some cattle. It's fifty miles around the road and only about thirty as the crow flies, so I decided to cut across. The snow had been deep during the winter and there were still thin layers of it in the brush. This made for heavy traveling across the flats and through the swales, so I held to the bare gravel ridges as much as possible.

It was almost noon by the sun when I topped out at the head of the five-mile draw. I stopped to rest for a few minutes and to raise my saddle so that air might cool Piute's sweaty back. He was grain fed and strong but the soft, wet soil was quite muddy in places, causing him to heat up considerably, and I didn't want to gall his back.

While resting there observing the country round about, I spotted several bunches of horses. Two bunches of seven were on the side of Nine Mile Mountain just below the cedar line. I guessed these would be mustangs, but they were too far away for me to chase this day. Three more bunches showed out on Toana Flat, and toward Murdock and North Spring I saw two more bunches. I didn't know the horses well enough to tell if they were wild. I turned toward Piute ready to mount when he threw up his head and looked to his right. Instead of climbing aboard I stepped out in front of him and saw the blue-gray Murphy stud standing about fifty yards away and looking at us. I backed up slowly and tightened my cinches. I was going to give the stud a run of some kind. Maybe I could hold the bunch together and put them into the Nine Mile field. There was a wing out from the side gate and it was always left open in the winter. Some horses wandered in there by themselves to get at the ryegrass when the snow was deep. If I failed to run them into the field I would try to get close enough to rope the Murphy stud.

From the saddle I could see the rest of the bunch coming out from behind three cedars to meet the dappled stallion. When they met I knew they would circle around each other a couple of times before starting to run. It was always the big sorrel mare that led, and, until they were pressed, the stud brought up the rear.

I rode south along the top of the ridge to see if I could influence the horses toward Nine Mile. When they went that way it pleased me very much. This gave me a chance at the field, and if the bunch came back at me they would be in the muddy soil of the brush while I traveled on the drier gravel ridge. As soon as the horses came out on top of the saddle north of me, the two bunches of mustangs on Nine Mile saw them and started north around the west side of the mountain. I thought for a moment that the blue-gray and his bunch might follow, but found they were just avoiding me a little and trying to skirt around me toward Toana Flat.

I made a loop in my rope and held it ready, knowing from experience that it's hard to guess what wild horses will do. As I galloped down the gentle slope of the ridge alongside the mustangs, I could see them struggling through the heavy mud in the low sage. Sometimes they sank in deep enough to almost bog down.

Although I waved my rope and hollered, they kept crowding toward me and I could see they were not going to go north; they would go in front of me or behind me but would not let me drive them where I wanted them to go.

The mares began to falter after the first mile of muddy running and the stud started to pass them one by one. It was going to be him and me. The stud hit a small wash and sunk into the mud nearly to his knees. He hesitated a moment before lunging out on top and continuing the race. I felt this faltering indicated he was weak from the rough winter and that I might get my chance at him soon.

Ahead of me a short distance I could see where the ridge I was on parted. It was my guess that this was where the stud would come out on the top and run with me.

It would be quite a race, side by side down the ridge. I was still holding Piute back and had never used all his speed. Maybe I could catch the stud on firmer ground but I would prefer the mud. It would slow the race down considerably.

Murphy skirted the ridge about like I expected and came out beside me only a few jumps from the point where the ridge separated. He crowded closer and closer to me, but when I raised my rope and swished it around my head, he turned right and fell off into the mud and brush of the shallow draw. I thought to turn Piute left and stay on the ridge, but he was not to be denied and barreled into the brush right behind the stud. When the stallion saw the opening on his left, for I was behind him now, he went straight across the draw to get more solid footing.

Piute was much stronger and ran with reckless abandon. His long strides took me up to the stud just as he was about to climb out on drier, gravelly ground. I threw my loop hard at his head, and when I saw it was a good catch, I hurried to jerk it up before the stud could step in the loop with his front feet.

Murphy was mine, too tired to fight much and no match for Piute when he did struggle. I didn't even dally the rope when I caught him, but followed him out onto the top of the ridge before I stopped him.

It was long after dark when I rode into the Gamble Ranch. They knew I was on my way because they had phoned the H-D. Though some of them wondered what had gone wrong, one man didn't wonder at all. Sid knew what could happen when you turn a cowboy loose in wild horse country.

Murphy was seven years old, a beautiful, chunky, dappled blue-gray. I broke him to ride and had him gentle when Ed Murphy came back on his next tour. All Ed said was, "I told you Piute could catch that dappled stud."

Ed was so right.

Hard and Fast

The sun was not yet up and the chill, early spring air made us shiver as we sat on our horses awaiting the day's assignment. We were riding for the Wine Cup cow outfit and were camped at the Eighteen Mile Ranch while we pushed the cattle off Thousand Springs Creek back to the hills where there was better grass. Otherwise they would hang along the fences wanting to return to the feed ground.

Six of us sat there humped over our saddles, hands tucked under the flaps of our bat-winged chaps and breath blowing fog in the cold morning air. We were eager for the orders that would allow us to gallop out and warm ourselves.

"Ben, you take Rusty and go down to the Twelve Mile. Move everything up toward the Crittenden. Parley, you gather along the ryegrass field from the narrows this way and take everything from around the spring. Drive them out on those mustang trails up the long draw toward Grassy Mountain. You'll be alone today, so be careful. Ned, John, and I will drive from here up the creek and start our cattle toward Rock Spring wash. We might come back over the end of Delno and charge at a mustang if we see one. Get your work done first and then have your fun."

That was Sid, the wagon boss, giving the orders. He was a real mustanger, and when he was in wild horse country he always rode his best horses. He was also a hard worker and drove his men all day and part of the night when necessary to get the job done. They loved him for it because he never asked a man to do anything he wouldn't do himself. When they had a chance for a little fun, like catching a mustang, he was all for it.

I was riding a chestnut sorrel horse with white legs and a blaze face. I called him Bally. He was chunky and heavy legged, certainly not a horse to win any races. Still, he could gallop well for about a hundred yards. I really liked him because he was good on a rope and always willing to do his best in any situation.

By sunrise, we were each working our assigned areas and were far enough apart that I couldn't even hear the others. This was no problem for me. I had ridden the range since I was nine, and now, at eighteen, I felt I could handle a situation as well as any man.

I gathered nearly fifty head of cattle in my area; about ten or twelve were calves. By the time I had convinced them they were to go up the draw toward Grassy Mountain, my horse was beginning to lather. It's quite a problem to ride both sides of a herd and then drop back and bring up the drags, especially when none of them is really anxious to go.

One old cow was determined to go back to the ranch. She just kept breaking away until finally I took down my rope and warped her a few times across the rump. She soon decided that was no fun at all and started looking for higher country. A little lashing sure made a leader out of her.

With her up front the rest started trailing along, so I rode off to the side and rested Bally for a few minutes. I shook my new saddle back into position and admired how it looked. That was my first new saddle and you can bet I was proud of it. I wiped the dust from it and pulled all the strings back in place. Only three months old, the saddle was not fitted well to the horse, so I had to cinch it down pretty tight to keep it on Bally's round back.

The cattle soon started grazing and walking along. I followed, yipping at them once in a while to let them know I was still there. Now and then I made a loop and flipped it at a calf or caught an old cow by the rump just for practice. I tied my rope to the horn so I wouldn't have to dally to pull it loose each time it tangled in a bush.

Grassy Mountain was about four miles up the draw. We let the cattle graze along the way, and it was past noon when we neared the pass and left them to scatter on the good feed. The cattle were contented, except the old cow that had led the way. She was nearly to the top of the pass and still climbing.

As she went out of sight over the summit, I saw a horse come out from the cedars on the Grassy Mountain side of the pass and head across toward a snowbank near the top of Delno. That horse was followed by several others—I counted eleven head. All of them were bays, browns, and blacks. Three I supposed were young studs because they followed at a short distance, probably whipped out of the herd by the old stud.

I was hoping it would be the blue roan stallion and his bunch. He was a pacer, a beautiful horse, and always a pleasure to see; but it wasn't him. While they were grazing their way up to the snowbank, I lifted my saddle again and reset it. The steep climb had caused it to slide back too far.

When I looked again the horses were gathering around the snowbank, apparently licking snow in lieu of drinking water. The three that I thought were young studs were still off to the side, rejected by the others. I stood by my horse and watched them for several minutes, not even dreaming I would have a chance to catch one. Then I decided to yell as loud as I could and see which way they would run. This I did, several times.

The old stud trotted off from the bunch and looked around. He was their sentinel. Bally and I stayed quiet and the stud could not spot us. When he turned and trotted back toward the bunch I could see he was restless. I yelled again, and this time all of them looked up. Then they started milling around, not sure which way to run.

Soon the lead mare, an old brown, started coming down the mountain toward me. The rest of the bunch followed with the old stud between the main herd and the three rejects.

Maybe I would have a chance. They were on trails that crossed just above me, leading to the ridges south of Grassy Mountain. If they continued to follow that course I would get a run at them.

Feverishly, I yanked at the latigo, and Bally looked around wondering why I pulled it so tight. I climbed in the saddle just as the brown mare came in sight above me. They had made their bid and wouldn't change course for any small reason. They were running strong, though I knew that the short run off the mountain had tired them. That early in the spring the grass was short and washy, so their strength would fade fast.

I yanked at my rope that lay coiled in front of me. The end was still tied to the saddle horn, the way it was during my horseplay as I trailed along behind the cattle. Nervously, I shook out a loop while moving in the direction of the brown mare.

The stud came into view, and he was no longer the last. His mane and tail stood out in the breeze stirred from his own speed as he crashed through the heavy sage in the swale of the draw, passing horse after horse. Every muscle and fiber of his body were straining to the utmost as he sped by me, much too far away for me to even attempt a throw. Six horses, including the three young studs, were still behind me and closing fast.

As I said before, Bally was not very fast, but he was willing. I quickly judged our position and decided that the black stud, third from the last, would top the ridge the same time I did, so I decided to concentrate on him. Bally was with me on this and I could feel the extra surge he made to put me where I could make my throw. We would meet the stud just at the edge of the sage where there was a little open ground before reaching the scrub cedars.

Now, I don't like to brag, but if I get close enough for my rope to reach, I don't worry about catching. So it was with that loop. The cast was good and I had the black mustang stud, just at the precise time when Bally could run no further. The rope was tied to the horn so I just let it run to the end, not even attempting to dally.

By the length of his mane and tail, I could see I had a young stud perhaps three years old. Any stud older than that would have been whipped from the bunch earlier and not be following along. Now that I had one roped, the old stud had only two to contend with. He should be grateful.

The steady pull on the rope soon choked the black and he toppled over, kicking his legs like a spoiled kid. I rode up on him and, when the rope came loose around his neck so he could breathe again, he immediately jumped up.

When the mustang got the glazed film off his eyes and saw me sitting on my horse beside him, he spooked and ran straight down the side of the short, steep ridge we were on. I missed my dally because of the excitement and when the stud hit the end of the rope, my horse was sideways to him. The shock jerked my new saddle clear over on Bally's side.

I didn't know whether to be happy or sad. If the rope hadn't been tied to the saddle horn I might have lost the rope. That could have been better than my present predicament. The saddle, way down on his side, frightened Bally, and he wanted to buck it loose. Still having a solid rope connection to five hundred pounds of wild mustang, I had to do something quickly.

When the young stud hit the end of the rope, it laid him out flat in the air and snapped his tail like a cracking bullwhip. Then he fell to the ground and stayed there like he was dead. I wondered if his neck might have broken, but didn't much care if it had. I had my own problems.

The surprise of the whole thing had thrown Bally out of balance. He nearly panicked with the heavy jerk that yanked him several feet down the hillside. Still tied to the mustang, and with the saddle almost halfway down his side, he just wanted to break loose from everything fastened to him.

Bally could see me still up above him. I spoke to him softly until he calmed down. Then I pulled the saddle upright using my left foot in the stirrup and my hand on the horn, throwing my weight to the side several times. It took a few minutes to get it back in position; then I tightened the latigo a few more holes so that scrawny broomtail wouldn't get away dragging my saddle.

I had plenty of time before the young stud staggered to his feet. He was quite subdued and wobbled haltingly to the bottom of the draw where he, Bally, and I went a few exciting rounds. I tussled and petted him until finally he followed me toward the ranch like a calf following its mother.

I was the only one who caught a mustang that day and so became the man of the hour. Bally received several respectful appraisals for his part in the capture.

"Hell, he's no bigger than a bag of peanuts," was one remark, so that was what we named him—Peanuts.

He broke out gentle and by the next spring he was fat and pretty. Still, I think that if he stood in the rain all day and was drenching wet, he would never weigh more than six hundred pounds.

That's one way to catch a mustang. Go out on the mountain, holler as loud as you can several times, and just rope one as it runs by. Easy.

Little Squaw

I saddled Little Squaw for my three young children: Ralph, age ten; Ted, age eight; and Lisa, age six, a child with dark, curly hair who chattered incessantly. Little Squaw was always patient with the children and seemed to enjoy their struggles and loving caresses as they traded places so each could have a turn at guiding. The saddle was old and lacked stirrups so the tiny feet would have no ready place to hang when the children fell, as they often did; but it was very important to have a turn in the saddle.

Little Squaw emitted a low sigh as he started to leave with a new rider at the reins, yet he needed no one to guide. He made about the same circle before returning to the platform for the eager riders to change places, two in the saddle and one hanging to the strings behind the cantle.

The little bay mustang had not always been so cooperative, so kindly, and so careful with his riders. My mind reflected back to the day I roped him some years before.

It was early spring and he was a scraggy-looking three-year-old stud with no mane and very little tail. While trapped in the deep snow of winter, he and two others had eaten each other's mane and tail hair to keep from starving. He was quite weak and Piute galloped up to him easily as he was nearing the top of Squaw Creek Pass. I threw my rope on him and held him without a dally. It was then I wondered if he was worth taking home.

Good feed and loving care made a pet out of Little Squaw, as we named him, and he broke out gentle and kind with a trace of mischief in his actions. Sometimes when least expected he would jump a ditch and buck real hard for about four jumps and then calm down gentle as a dog.

One day when I was poppin' brush near Red Point there was a yearling that persisted in running back into the heavy thickets. I searched it out several times, even traveling on foot part way to keep it coming. When we came to an opening in the brushy draw I thought I might rope the yearling and make it wild enough so it would not tease along as it was doing.

I tied my rope and made a pass. Everything was in my favor and I was closing on the animal to make my shot. Round and round I swung the loop and as I leaned over and cast, Little Squaw sucked back under me and bucked me off. It was downright humiliating. That little mustang only weighed about eight hundred pounds and was gentle, very gentle. Everyone knew that. What could I tell them at the ranch?

Well, I picked myself up and walked over to Little Squaw, who was standing quietly near the edge of the heavy brush. We would have it out once and for all. I'd show that runt of a mustang who was boss. I mounted up and spurred him from shoulder to tail—but he wouldn't buck. He wouldn't do anything but stand quietly and take his punishment. All of a sudden I was ashamed to be so cruel and I brushed and rubbed the spur marks, petting Little Squaw and confessing it was right that he should buck me off.

The squabble between Little Squaw and me was my secret, and I meant to have some fun from it before the summer was over. As we trailed cattle from place to place, branded calves, and worked the herd, I told the others of Little Squaw's gentle nature. He followed me with the reins over the horn and nipped at an old slow cow now and then as a dog might do. I took every opportunity to show how tame and trustworthy my mustang was, and it soon paid off. Everyone was noticing, especially Dusty Rhodes, a new hand of a few weeks. As his horses were undependable, he longed for one he could really trust. Each day I rode Little Squaw, Dusty received full benefit of my deception, and one day he asked if I would trade him for any of his.

"No, Dusty, I think not. You don't have a horse I really like, but I might take one of the new broncs and let you have Little Squaw if you get approval from the boss."

"I'll talk to him today. I sure need a dependable horse." Dusty was eager to obtain Little Squaw. I almost felt a twinge of guilt but I quickly brushed it aside. The trade was made and secretly I looked forward to the day when Little Squaw would show his true dependability, as I knew he would.

It was weaning time and ten of us were enjoying some lively fun cutting the calves from their mothers. We put them out in a corner of the big upper meadow before taking them to the weaning trap, an area fenced with net wire built especially to hold the four- to six-month-old calves. We had nearly a hundred cut to one side with a half dozen cows.

"Let's take them before we get too many to handle!" Sid called, and except for two cowboys who stayed to hold the cows, we all converged on the weaners.

It was a lively ride to the weaning trap and a busy time to get the mixed-up, bawling calves through the gate. Time after time a calf or two or three would break away and have to be circled and brought back. Finally there were fewer than ten left to put through the gate.

"Rope 'em!" Sid called out.

Each man already had his rope ready and the fun began. I watched Dusty let one by and swing his rope for the catch—but he didn't get his loop away. Little Squaw sucked under him, as he had done with me, laying Dusty full out on his back. I was ready to catch Little Squaw and chuckled to myself as I made a good throw with my loop.

A few more calves came out of the trap to join us and we had calves and cowboys all over the area. Dusty thanked me, I think, and mounted. He built a loop as he galloped toward a big heifer calf that was trying to go back to her mother. I couldn't find a calf to rope because my eyes kept following Dusty.

He sat straighter in the saddle and threw a faster loop this second time, but Little Squaw was running his hesitating step and as the rope left Dusty's hand, Little Squaw swapped ends and started bucking back and to the left. Dusty was not solid in the saddle after the first jump; and after the fourth or fifth, he left the saddle like he had been sucked off with a suction cup. Little Squaw was standing still by the time Dusty quit rattling on the ground.

Dusty pulled himself together slowly. He'd hit the ground hard and his breath was taken away. I watched him gather in his hat, slap it against his chapped leg to dust it off, and pull it tight on his head so his eyes barely peeked out from under the brim. He meant to have a showdown with Little Squaw. Maybe once was all right but twice was too much. I didn't say anything to explain because I didn't think it was any of my business.

Well, Dusty couldn't get even one jump out of Little Squaw either. Like he had been with me, that crafty mustang stood quietly and took the whipping and spurring and hollering and cussing that Dusty dished out. He knew what he could do and when to do it and this was not the time.

I watched Little Squaw change hands several times. That gentle, kind little mustang followed each rider like a dog until the precise time the cowboy got himself far enough off balance. At that moment Little Squaw turned into a twisting, spinning, bucking horse for the few jumps it took to unload his rider. As soon as the rider hit the ground it was over. More often than not, Little Squaw just stood and waited to be caught. Once in a while he would make a half-hearted effort to run away, but he was easily captured.

It's quite probable that Little Squaw bucked off every cowboy that ever rode him for any length of time, each one in the same easy, efficient manner: he'd wait until the moment the cowboy was off balance and suck away, leaving him in space without his saddle.

The last time I remember him doing that was when several of us were pushing cattle up through the heavy brush toward summer camp. We came upon a maverick calf near old enough to be weaned and we decided to brand it so it wouldn't be lost if the mother should wean it before fall.

Ray was topped out on Little Squaw and had a new rope. He was a hard and fast man and claimed to come out of Texas, which didn't mean much. A lot of men were in and out of Texas as they searched for or moved from a job cowboying or line riding.

Ray was a pretty fair rider and extra good with a rope, and he'd heard Little Squaw would try him if the proper opportunity came. After pulling his cinch tight, Ray mounted and shook out a loop. I sort of eased the big maverick around toward Ray, as I wanted to see the action.

Little Squaw cut off to the side a couple times when Ray faked a throw, but he didn't buck. After several passes Little Squaw calmed down and when the calf came by again, Ray made his bid. He spurred Little Squaw out toward the calf and had a good, clear field for a short distance before they would enter some larger brush. Ray was just a little too anxious to make the catch while still in the clearing, and that was his downfall. Little Squaw was doing his hesitating run, and Ray was urging with rein and spur, watching the calf get closer and closer to the brush. Little Squaw was not going to put out effort enough to get that other jump closer, so Ray leaned out and threw hard. Just then Little Squaw ducked back, the rope missed, and after four hard, spinning jumps, Ray was flat on the ground.

I knew exactly how he felt, I guess, but not really. Ray was quiet the rest of the day, and that night he rolled up his bed, tossed it in the rumble seat of his little Ford, packed up his saddle and gear, and headed for town. I saw him about a month later dealing blackjack in a casino in Elko. He said if he couldn't ride a kid pony like Little Squaw, it was time to quit.

A Mustang Named Rat

"Now, what did you want to catch a thing like that for?" Ben was about as disgusted as a man could be. "Those three nice young studs in the bunch and you come up with this. Let's cut his throat and leave him here in the brush and not say we caught him. Maybe no one will find out."

Ben was lambasting me for roping a rattailed brown stud that was as ugly as any horse I could ever remember seeing. We had worked all morning to get in the right place to make a good run on a bunch of ten mustangs but came up short. Ben's horse fell in a sharp wash and took him clear out of the race and, although I was among the horses for a couple of minutes, the scrub cedars and serviceberry bushes allowed me only one opportunity and I took it: the ugly, rattailed, brown stud.

I was riding my big white horse, Flora, and he handled the mustang on the rope like he was a weaner calf. Love and pride swelled inside me for this fine saddle horse. His speed was not great, but his ability and willingness were exceptional. I let him play the stud on the rope for a few minutes while I thought of an answer for Ben, which wouldn't be easy. That brown stud was ugly as sin.

"Sure hate to go in empty-handed, Ben," I ventured, hesitating to even look Ben in the eye. He was right and I knew it, we would be much better off without the stud. "He does have good feet, Ben."

"Yes, his feet are good and his legs are reasonably straight, but from there on he's a disaster. Look at those little hog eyes with the heavy brows and . . . and . . . those pin ears that turn in at the top. He'll be mean to break, I tell ya. I sure don't want him in my string. Not even to pack my bed." Ben went on describing the horse, "Heavy jaws, ewe neck, swayback, hips you could hang your hat on—and that tail is a beaut. You can have him. He's not for me." Ben was still mumbling as he rode around behind the stud.

The mustang, coming off a choking spree, darted toward Flora and me. His ears were laid back and he showed fight in his action.

"Look out!" Ben called.

I deftly flipped the dallies off the saddle horn, looped a couple coils from the slack rope into my left hand, turned Flora so his rump protected me from the teeth of the stud, and, as the stud passed by, I wrapped the rope three times around the saddle horn. Three dallies would hold a bull and that's what I needed. I felt Flora lean, anticipating the jerk when the mustang would hit the end of the rope, and I threw my weight into the off stirrup to aid him.

The stud ran out of rope as he was leaping, but the continued thrust of his hind legs snapped him out level about four feet off the ground. He came down—kerwhump! The mustang lay quiet in the brush.

"Saved yer life there. Ya owe me one!" Ben called.

"Fair enough, Ben!" I said. "You can have the stud. That would more than make us even."

"No, thanks! I'd rather ya owe me. I tell ya, I don't want that ill-shaped stud. Not now, or ever."

Well, we took the stud in to the Eccles Ranch where the cow wagon was camped and took a good ribbing from the boys. Finally the wagon boss said, "You brought him in, Parley. You'll have to ride him."

I put a hackamore on him and tied him to the fence in the corral close enough to the trough so he could get water and high enough so he wouldn't get a leg over the lead rope. I tucked a few handfuls of hay into the fence, though I was sure the mustang stud wouldn't know what it was. We looked at his teeth and guessed him to be five years old.

The next day I worked with him all day long. Toward evening I was able to guide him around the corral. Before turning him loose for the night, Ben and I branded and castrated him, not caring if he lived or died.

He was there the next morning, though, very much alive, and for the next ten days he and I spent much time together. The soreness from his castration passed slowly, and he was ready to travel when we moved the wagon. There was much excitement for the next several days as the mustang, now known as "the Rat," learned to stay with the saddle horses, became acquainted with the various new sights and sounds of the cow outfit, and found his own place in the rope corral.

When I was able to get back to the Rat he had become belligerent and stubborn. He had been around humans long enough to have no fear, and was defiant of everything I asked of him.

He wouldn't lead; he wouldn't turn; he would sulk and buck and sulk again. I gave up riding the Rat altogether and used him only to pack my bedroll from time to time. This, however, couldn't continue. Having grown up alongside my father, who broke every reluctant or spoiled horse in the territory, I wasn't about to let this one get the best of me.

We came in from a short circle one day, and the boss said we could have the rest of the day to do what needed to be done. Some put shoes on their horses or mended their gear, but the pressing item for me was Rat and his worsening nasty attitude.

I dumped my gunnysack and found the thin, spot-cord cotton rope I needed to fashion a sort of war bridle for my ratty mustang. I laced the rope through one ring on my snaffle bit and then ran it across the top of the Rat's head close behind his ears and down through the other ring of the bit. Then I tied my reins to the rope. That gave me good leverage on the nerve that is close to the surface behind any animal's ears.

Rat and I fought face-to-face on the ground for some time. When he resisted I used a surging action on the reins to encourage him to concede. I soon had him so he would willingly lead anywhere. When I had him responsive to my touch on the reins, I tightened the cinch and mounted up. Facing into a corner of a small willow corral, Rat waited quietly until I was set and had pulled on the rein to turn him down the fence. At first he didn't respond, and when I gave a quick surge he shuddered as if struck on the head with a pole.

I kicked loose from my stirrups so I could clear him if he fell, but he didn't fall. Instead he came out of that corner bucking and squealing, releasing all of his pent-up fury against me.

On the second jump I caught one stirrup, and then hooked the other one with my toe on the third. Rat was sprawled out like he might fall apart, and I could see he was blind to the fence in front of him. I jerked hard on the reins as we plowed into the fence. We hit hard, with Rat's head banging directly into a post. He sat down, his frame shaking and quivering. I watched for him to roll over on one side but he struggled to his feet, so I remained in the saddle determined to finish the battle.

I spoke to him quietly, gently tightening the reins to see if he would respond. Carefully, almost reluctantly, he stepped to the side, moving as though he expected the fence to crash down on his head again. The bucking and falling experience was definitely in my favor. Rat was not sure the happenings were not my doing. I took full advantage of the situation, and Rat responded to my every request until the day I turned him back into the cavy as a broken saddle horse.

Right at that time a new man hired on and drew Rat as one of his string. A few days later he walked into camp and Rat showed up among the cavy carrying the saddle and dragging the bridle reins. "He sort of came apart and I thought he was going to fall. I kicked loose and he bucked me off before I could get set." The new hand made no more excuse than that.

Over the next two years Rat did this to four different riders and built quite a reputation for himself. There were times when I wondered if I could ride him, but I was not real anxious to try.

One day, late in September, a slim, long-legged cowboy hired on. He was quiet and not much concerned about others around him. He did his work well and rode the horses given him without remark, until he was given Rat.

"We're short on horseflesh, Slim. You won't mind riding the Rat will you? Some have had trouble with him," so said the boss one dark, early morning.

"Any of them, boss. Any of them."

The day was long and the country rough. It was two P.M. before any riders showed at the branding ground and much later before the calves were branded and the beef cut out. Slim and Rat didn't show until just after sundown and then it was Slim, carrying his saddle and gear. There was no Rat.

"Run into problems?" the boss asked.

"Not much of a problem," Slim said. "Rat fell and broke his leg and I had to destroy him. I didn't have a gun so I just cut his throat. He was certainly a miserable horse wasn't he, Sid? Not exactly trustworthy. You won't really miss him much, will you?"

"We've wished this would happen to the Rat, never really believing it could. It's sort of a relief to have him gone. You all right, Slim?"

The days went by and Slim proved an excellent cowboy. No one ever checked to see if he always told the truth.

The Killer

My saddle horse, Starlight, snorted and sidled around the dead colt, resisting my coaxing to move closer so I could determine more readily what had killed the young animal. I guessed the colt to be about ten days old, large enough to follow its mother almost anywhere. Judging from the condition of the mare standing nearby, periodically nickering for her baby and bag tight with milk, I was certain she was not the problem. Her strong mothering instinct would probably keep her near the dead colt for several days.

For some distance around, the ground was cut with deep horse tracks, indicating the mare had fought hard for her offspring. This was the third colt I had found dead in this area since last spring. The other colts each had had a broken neck, and from the looks of the marks on this one, its neck was broken also. I pondered the possiblities. A cougar would either eat the colt or bury it. It is not an animal that kills from lust, but rather when it is hungry. And a wolf would go for the throat instead of the top of the neck.

As the mother came closer to smell her colt again, I saw that her neck had been bitten several times between the withers and the crest. A stallion will do that sometimes to put another horse in its place or to bring a mare into submission, but never to the extent of injury this mare had received.

My mind flashed back to last spring when I was riding here on Bovine Mountain a little farther up the north side in a basin called Horse Heaven. There were three bunches of horses in the basin that day, and all were branded except for a black stallion I had never seen before and a mare mule about three or four years old. The stallion and the mule were wild and stayed with the gentler horses only long enough for me to see they were unbranded before running from the mountain. I watched that day as they galloped down the long ridge toward the granite rock spires we called the Needles before riding around the gentle horses and banding them together in preparation for taking them home.

As I came out on top of a high knoll I scanned the lower country and saw dust in the edge of the flat and two small black dots I supposed were the horse and mule. I guessed they were going to Watercress Spring, miles out into the desert.

In my mind I considered the experience of that day. I surmised that possibly the wild ones had been chased from Hogup Mountain which, as I looked, showed blue in the distance. I knew cowboys who had run mustangs on Hogup and it was certainly possible some could be scared off into the desert and come across to Bovine Mountain.

I stepped down by the dead colt to examine for predator tracks. While thus engaged, I saw the mare look up toward the ridge in back of me at that same wild mule, brown over most of her body and a nose that was gray, almost white. She emitted a raspy call as only a mule can do, slightly refined from a jackass or burro. Her long ears flopped forward and back a few times as she shook her head and stamped a front foot, apparently determining what to do.

I crouched close under my horse and watched as the mule laid her ears back, bared her teeth, and charged, not at me as I hunkered down by the dead colt, but at the mare who was standing several yards to one side.

The mare screamed a cry of desperation and whirled her rump toward the mule, kicking ferociously, but it was only a couple of minutes before the mule crowded in and sunk her teeth into the top of the mare's neck. I knew immediately that I had found the killer.

Quickly I mounted Starlight and charged toward the pair. The mare was down on her knees and in a desperate circumstance, the mule hanging on tenaciously, determined to finish her victim in spite of my presence. I whipped the mule with my heavy rawhide quirt and yelled as loud as I could, but the mare went down on her side before the mule loosened her death grip and looked at me while working the hair free from her foaming mouth. I wondered if I might be next, from the way her glazed eyes stared at me. My quirt snapped as I cracked it against my chap leg, and the mule whirled away and trotted back to the top of the ridge. It was then I noticed the black stud standing against the skyline and the mule walked up and posed beside him. They were an ominous-looking pair invading a new territory, my territory, and I was going to do what was necessary to protect my own.

The mare lay for awhile before struggling to her feet. She was weak and staggering and it took me the rest of the day to coax her off the mountain and to the pasture at Pucket Spring. I put her inside the field where she would be protected from further abuse and closed the gate.

I saw some horses in the stockade corral over by the spring about a quarter mile south of me and rode over to see what was going on. Smoke was coming from the chimney of a sheep camp near the spring. Someone had fired up the stove to cook dinner. This thought reminded me that I hadn't eaten since daylight, and my stomach automatically rumbled its indignation.

A horse whinnied high up the ridge toward Rocky Pass, and as I looked I saw a rider on a bay horse following along the fence line. He would be checking for breaks and places laid flat by the winter drifts.

I guessed it was my good friend, Jesse James, and that he'd shut his saddle horses in the corral until he was sure the fence would hold them in the pasture. As I watched the rider he looked even more like Jesse's slight, slouched form. He was small and wiry and rode all over his horse, always shifting from one position to another. He appeared to be tempting the horse to hang him on a bush as they passed, but when the need came he could ride any kind of bronc and was especially good on the range.

I found my cousin Bart at the camp fixing the meal. There were four saddle horses in the corral and a big bay mule. The mule had sweat marks from carrying a pack and was the largest mule I had ever seen. The saddle horses were dwarfed by his enormous size.

"Hello, the camp!" I called.

"Hello, yourself," Bart said, poking his head out of the door.

"How are you, Bart? I thought your camp was north of here."

"It is. We're camped at Sickle Springs and have the sheep on Ingham Mountain. I came down with Jesse to help ride a couple of days for a change."

"I can see Jesse up on the ridge. Thought he might be riding the fence."

"Yup. That's him. Said he'd check the fence while I put lunch together. Better light and have some bacon and eggs with us."

"How did he ever carry eggs over here on a pack mule?"

"He broke them into a peanut butter jar. Filled it tight to the lid and they traveled pretty good. Much better than I would have expected."

"Boy, there's a way to do everything if you can think of it."

I heard a loud whoop from Jesse and saw him coming off the hill at full gallop in hot pursuit of two big buck deer. They were jumping crooked, not sure which way was best, and Jesse was at the height of his glory, screaming as loud as he could. About a hundred yards above the spring one buck veered to the left and the other to the right. They were out of sight by the time the laughing Jesse rode into camp.

"Hello, Jesse. Why didn't you rope one?" I said as he rode up facing me.

"I would have but I had no place to keep him. I'll come back this fall and take one of them home."

"You don't hunt this far south do you, Jesse? I thought you stayed with the Red Butte country."

"I'd come down here for one of those big ones. They were sure nice and fat. What brings you over here, Parley? After some of your horses?"

"I've been branding a few colts, Jesse, and taking some mares over to Keg Springs to be with the stud. I ran into a funny deal today. Something killed a colt belonging to that mare I put into the field."

"I wondered why you put her in."

"Have you heard of a black mustang stud that runs with a wild, unbranded brown mule with a white nose? They don't belong here. May have come from Hogup or the Watercress, Kelton country. I ran into them first time last spring and had no chance to bring them in. Today I saw them again. The mule is about five or six and a killer. She kills colts especially and today she nearly killed the mare I brought in. She gets them by the cord of the neck and hangs on 'til they die. I have to get her off the range somehow or else not raise any colts here."

Jesse listened as he turned his horses loose to graze in the pasture. "I'll bet they're the ones the Black brothers were talking about. The Blacks ran mustangs on Hogup for a couple of months, a year ago last fall. They water trapped some and a lot of the horses moved off the mountain. They talked about a mule and a black stud. Even had them in the corral once, but the mule killed one of their saddle horses. They dragged her out of the corral and were going to cut her throat, but she bit that old seagrass rope a few times and broke it. She got away, and somehow the stud went with her. You know how hard it is to get the pure truth out of some of these stories. I bet it's the same two animals though. They definitely said a mule and black stud. The mule would be five this spring and the stud six, the way they figured them."

"I could knock them off with my rifle if you want me to, Parley," Bart put in.

"That may be the safest and surest way to go, Parley," Jesse added.

"If the stud is only six years old, he would break out to be a nice saddle horse. I'd really like to try a run at them first. The mule is no concern but I hate to waste a good horse."

"Tell you what," Jesse said. "If we can put them in the pasture with a bunch of horses and corral them as the Black brothers did, we could catch that miserable mule and neck her to old Joe. That's my big pack mule. He's big enough and mean enough to handle her with no problem. I'll take her home and do something with her. You'll never see her on the range again, I'll promise you that. You can have the black stud, Parley. He's too old for me to break gentle. I just don't have work enough to keep him busy."

So it was decided that on the morrow we would gather the horses Jesse wanted and put them in the pasture. The second day we would try for the black stallion and the wild mule.

I rode to my camp at Keg Springs that night with a much lighter heart than I had earlier when bending over the dead colt. Deep within me a good feeling made me think the wild mule was about at the end of her killing spree, and maybe I would get a good saddle horse out of the deal to take the place of the three dead colts.

The next morning I rolled a heavy hackamore and rope in my jacket and tied it on the back of my saddle. That was for the black stud. I was sure we would capture him and I would neck him to one of my big work mares that ranged near Pucket Springs. At least I thought it best to be prepared.

The day went smoothly for me as I gathered the horses from Mogul to Pucket and held them in a bunch awaiting Jesse and Bart. I had about fifty head, too many for the pasture or the corral, but they were all gentle and if I was careful I could sluff some of them off and hold only the ones we wanted.

I was about to do this when I saw a big dust cloud in the draw leading from Horse Heaven. Looking closer I could see three or four bunches of horses filtering through the trees and crowding the trail toward Pucket Spring. They were running faster than usual, and I wondered if by chance the mule and stud were with them.

I rounded up the horses I had and pushed them toward the spring where all of the horses would come together. I opened the gate to the pasture just in case and rode out on the trails toward the Needles. If the wild stud was in the bunch I was sure he would try to get away on these trails. I anxiously awaited the arrival of the horses, wondering what sort of race I would have. Rope in hand, I was ready for any event.

The horses burst through the edge of the trees into the wide sagebrush draw in one close bunch. The mule was there, running beside a mare and colt along the edge of the bunch. She was stalking another victim, I thought, and this one would be her undoing, because while she was intent on the colt we would lead her quietly to the corral and a noose. I doubted the black stud would leave alone unless we crowded him. He was running in the center of the bunch near the mule.

After a short race across the draw we skirted a cedar-covered ridge and the horses all gathered at the spring. Some wanted to drink while others milled around getting acquainted. I called to Jesse and Bart telling them the gate to the pasture was open. We quietly maneuvered the horses into the pasture and closed the gate. Some of them wanted more to drink, so it was easy to get them to go back toward the spring and the corral.

"The mule is stuck on the bay mare and colt and the stud is staying close to the mule. If they will go in the corral with a small bunch we might cut them off and close the gate." I was not talking loudly, because we were all close together.

"Good thinking," Bart said.

"Don't crowd too quick or we might lose 'em. Looks to me like they're real nervous," Jesse added, reading their actions and knowing what we might expect. The black stud came around the outside of the bunch several times, only to duck back into the middle for protection. I was glad the Black brothers had acquainted him with the corral. He wasn't as spooky as a horse that had never been inside a fence. Finally our patience paid off and the right opportunity came for us to push them into the corral. We rode our horses inside and closed the gate. They were ours now; no horse could jump over the high stockade fence.

We had a terrible time with the wild mule. It's almost impossible to choke a mule down, and she kicked the rope off her front feet time after time. Finally we were able to subdue her with a half hitch along with the loop.

The wild mule was much smaller than the big pack mule and may not have been as mean. That big mule put the wild one in her place with a kick to the belly with both hind feet. Those who understand mules know they don't kick for fun—they kick at a target. After another kicking tussel and a bite on the shoulder that took out a wad of hair, the wild mule willingly followed the pack mule.

I caught my big gray work mare, Pearl, and after leading her out of the bunch so she wouldn't get tromped by the running horses, I roped the black stallion. He fought ferociously, biting at the rope, kicking and pawing at the air. After choking down several times he weakened considerably and I crowded him against the fence and placed the hackamore on him. Jesse brought Pearl up behind us and we maneuvered her between the stud and me and then tied the rope around Pearl's neck to fasten her and the stud together on about three feet of rope. Called necking them together, this forced the wild animal to travel the same speed and direction as the gentle horse, making him easier to handle.

Bart and Jesse helped me line my horses out toward home and I had no trouble at all with the wild stud. He and Pearl soon learned to travel together, and, after adjusting to his restricted travel, he had no inclination to try an escape.

I named him Raven to fit his black color, broke him to ride, and enjoyed his easy-traveling gait for two years before I sold him. Jesse took the mule home partially broken to lead. He sold her to a farmer near Burley, Idaho, who wanted a good work animal to pull his plow.

Ridge Runnin' Roan

The sun was coming up to a clear sky as we rode into the saddle of Squaw Creek Pass. A red glow daintily caressed the tip of Squaw Peak to the north of us and then spread over the entire range to usher in a beautiful spring day.

I was riding for the Wine Cup cow outfit, gathering horses for branding and breaking. My two companions were Gilbert and Sid. Gilbert, a slight, stoop-shouldered man with steel-gray eyes and a week-old beard that was more gray than black, sat quietly on a big, red sorrel horse called Vinegar. He was searching the area round about, deep concentration showing on his countenance. He didn't really expect to see the horses he wanted, but he was studying in his mind where they might be.

Sid was a tall, slim, square-jawed fellow with bushy eyebrows and a prominent nose. He was adjusting the front cinch on Rudy, his tall bay saddle horse. Rudy was shallow on each side of his withers and the saddle rode forward a little, placing the front cinch of the double-rig Hamley close to the front leg.

Both men wore small Stetson hats pulled close over their eyes. They knew that if you lost your hat while running wild horses it might be a long ride back to find it.

Less than half their age and with limited experience, I was the kid in the group. Yet they catered to me, tolerated my mistakes, and at times accepted my humble judgment. Most often I listened and did what I was told.

"Fix the cinch, Sid?" Gilbert broke from his own deep thought.

"I think so. I let the billet down a hole and that puts the cinch ring up about three inches. At least it will wear in a new place." Sid finished tightening his latigo and mounted.

"I can think of only five horses north of Maverick Pass that we haven't gathered," Gilbert was studying again. "That blue roan ridge runner, a black mare with a big star on her forehead, and those three brown geldings we lost yesterday. They'll all run like scalded dogs." Gilbert described everything that was wild as running like a scalded dog.

"Ya, they'll run all right, but if we can put them north around Squaw Creek Mountain they'll run into our day herd. We have nearly four hundred horses in that bunch so the wild ones should stop with them." Sid had handled many wild horses and knew what they would do in just about any situation. If we could get the five animals mentioned, all the horses from Squaw Creek Mountain would be gathered. This had not been accomplished in the last five years.

I shifted a little in my saddle to get a better view of Maverick Pass and the several ridges that extended like fingers toward Independence Valley. The large granite rocks, cedars, and piñon pines lining the north wall of the pass were confined to the upper ends of the ridges. Below the rocks there was only a scattering of cedars and black sage.

I watched the dust kick up from one of the few cars that traveled Maverick Pass. It was clipping along at about thirty miles an hour, which was considered a safe speed. There were no big trucks on the road at all, since the railroad handled all the heavy, distance freighting. I didn't know this at the time we were there, however; I was intent on observing things at hand.

"Think you can keep up to us, kid?" Gilbert asked. "That mustang of yours is not very big."

I was riding a red sorrel called Peoho, a desert mustang weighing about nine hundred pounds. He looked almost like a yearling next to the horses Gilbert and Sid rode.

"He's not very big, Gilbert," I said in agreement, "but he can stick with many bigger horses."

"Peoho," Gilbert said thoughtfully. "It was four years ago when we caught him over in Silver Zone Pass. Machach was with us. He's the one who put that handle on him. Said he stuck like a louse so he named him Peoho, the little louse. He's a good horse all right. I was just kiddin' a little." Machach was a Mexican cowboy who rode for an outfit in Clover Valley a few miles to the west of us.

"Ya, he's an extra good horse for a mustang," Sid added. "He'll bring you home if it's at all possible."

I patted Peoho's neck affectionately. He was one of my choice saddle horses and I was confident in his abilities.

"Where should we look first?" I asked.

"I think we should ride the country toward Maverick, don't you, Gilbert?" Sid asked, heading in that direction.

"Looks like that's our best bet, Sid," Gilbert replied, then turned to me and asked, "What do you think, kid?"

I was trying hard to come up with a good answer without simply agreeing with their decision, when I saw what I thought was a horse grazing out from among the rocks far to the south.

"I believe you're right. In fact, I think I can see a horse near the rocks about four ridges south. It might be a rock, but I thought it moved."

"Good eyes, kid. Good eyes." Gilbert stirred with excitement. "That's the roan sure as shootin', and the others are under the trees just beyond him." Sid was quick to see what we were looking at and began planning a strategy.

Sid would ride the side of the mountain. Gilbert was to stay below him at the edge of the low ridges and I would start the horses. If our plan worked, I would run the horses out onto the flat along the highway to the trails that led to Holburn Spring and turn them north to the spring, and then east along the railroad. All the time I was doing this, Gilbert and Sid would be high enough on the mountain to watch the race. If I was able to turn the horses east along the railroad I could pull up and they would take them around the north of Squaw Creek Mountain to the day herd. It all sounded so easy.

I planned my approach to the horses in my favor and ran them to the flat and turned them north. Peoho was running strong, and I was certain my part of the race was going to be a snap. The five wild horses apparently wanted to go the direction I guided them. At any rate, they didn't give me any serious contest.

We galloped into Holburn Spring on the heavily traveled trails from the south, the wild horses following the trails without hesitation. About a quarter mile from the spring they veered toward Squaw Creek Mountain. I had to turn them one more time. Peoho was eager to run, so I slackened the reins and let him go. We passed the four dark-colored horses as they turned toward the railroad; they were running in the right direction.

The roan was determined to go back to the mountain, and we had a neck-and-neck race for some distance. A short while before this, I had seen Sid and Gilbert; they would get the dark horses all right, but the roan would be long gone if I couldn't turn him this one time.

I asked Peoho for a little more speed and he responded. We were slightly ahead of the roan when I saw him falter. Now if he only didn't cut out behind me. We came up fast on a small area of sharp rocks, invisible from any distance or I would have guided around them. I had to slow down or lose the roan. I knew Peoho should have his head free to pick his footing in the rocks, but I also knew if I didn't slow it would be too late.

I pulled up on the reins as we hit the rocks. Peoho scrambled for good footing and though he didn't fall, he did flounder about. I looked for the roan ridge runner and he had gone behind me and back toward the ridges near Maverick Pass. I stopped and watched him for a short time. He was certainly a beautiful animal and looked his best as he galloped through the sage still wild and free.

Peoho limped when I turned him back toward the other horses, and I dismounted and checked his foot to see if he had a rock wedged in his shoe or a bruised heel. I also checked his leg for tenderness and determined that he had torn or broken something in his pastern, someplace between his fetlock and the coffin joint at the top of the hoof.

My immediate thought was that he was ruined and would have to be destroyed. Leading him around a few steps, I could see that he was reluctant to put any weight on the foot. I figured he was too lame to go back to camp even if I didn't destroy him, and I studied for some time wondering what would be best for the horse. It was completely against my wishes to leave him alive if he might starve to death because he was unable to get feed, so I set about trying to decide how I could take his life. There were only two alternatives—choke him with a rope or cut his jugular vein with a knife. The latter is what I decided to do.

I pulled my saddle and laid it on the ground, placing the saddle blankets over it. Peoho nuzzled me as I walked around him patting and rubbing his beautiful red sorrel body. What a fine, honest saddle horse! My hands shook as I took my knife from the pocket of my chaps. I hated to do what I had decided. I opened the long, thin blade of my knife and stroked it a few times against the leg of my chaps. When I tested the blade against my arm it cut the hair quick and clean. It was as sharp as a razor.

I pushed Peoho's head away from me so I could see the pulse of the heartbeat in his jugular. I thought it wouldn't take the full length of the blade so I tightened my thumb and forefinger about halfway up, holding the rest of the knife in the palm of my hand. Peoho had a curl in his hair like in the crown of your head, and it was in about the right place along his throat. There the skin would be bare and the sharp blade could penetrate more easily.

Why had I tried so hard to turn the roan horse? Why hadn't I just let him pass? I would much rather have Peoho with four good legs than the roan any day. My foolish mistake had cost me a good saddle horse, and my whole body ached at the thought of it.

I made a determined move toward the horse. I pushed his head away from me again so I wouldn't have to look in his eye and raised the razor-sharp blade. Right at the curl of the hair directly over the jugular vein, I thought. One quick movement and it would be over. A hard way to go, but better than starving to death. I placed the heel of my hand on his neck to steady the knife and made ready. I paused a long moment—and I couldn't do it.

I just couldn't do it. Quickly I closed the knife and slipped it into my chap pocket to put temptation out of sight. Again I walked around him, petting and loving him with fond caresses. Peoho knew something was wrong and nickered to show his trust in me. I couldn't fail him now. There must be a way out.

My horse needed easy access to grass and water, two commodities not generally found together on the range. Grass close to water is the first to be plucked and eaten. But if there was little water it might not attract many animals. I thought of a small spring a short distance away; that was where I determined to leave Peoho. He was almost carrying his foot now, and it took what seemed like hours to get to the spring.

There was a muddy strip about six feet wide and two hundred feet long. A small stream of water puddled at the head and then ran from track to track down the strip. There was enough grass for a few days. I stroked Peoho's neck a few times, telling him softly how sorry I was for the incident that had placed us in this unhappy situation. I promised him that the roan ridge runner would pay—that I would catch him and subdue his wild, reckless spirit and place him under my saddle.

I turned Peoho loose and he drank from the clear water, and then walked out into the mud. I picked up my saddle, bridle, and blankets and walked toward camp knowing that the mud would draw the fever and swelling from the injured leg. That was all I could do for Peoho.

It took until nearly dark to walk the distance back to Squaw Creek carrying my riding tack. Riding boots, chaps, and spurs are never conducive to easy walking. Every step I took made me more determined to catch the ridge runner and make him take the place of my beloved Peoho.

Sid and Gilbert were graining the saddle horses when I walked into camp.

"Where's your horse?" Sid asked.

"I ran into a mess of sharp rocks and he broke something in his pastern on the right leg. I had to leave him."

"We could see something went wrong when the roan went back to the ridges," Gilbert interjected, and then asked, "Is he bad or will he be all right after he heals?"

"I think he's done for. I left him in the little mud spring out from Holburn and he was content not to walk at all. I even thought of cutting his throat but didn't have the courage."

"He'll probably be all right," Sid said. "The mud will keep the fever down and if he doesn't get infection he'll live. More than likely he'll grow a club foot and be able to get around, but he may never be good to ride again."

"I'd like to get that roan to take Peoho's place. He's really the one behind all this bad luck. Can we try him again tomorrow?" I asked, knowing we had only one more day to ride the range before working the horses.

Gilbert lifted his sweat-blackened, gray Stetson and scratched his tousled hair. "We could let you try him again tomorrow, kid," he said. "We have everything else from Squaw Creek Mountain. There's five young geldings in Collar and Elbow Sid and I want to bring in if we can, but you can tackle the roan again if you want. That's all right with you isn't it, Sid?"

"Sure, have at him. If I were you I think I'd ride Dean. He can run an ordinary horse to death. Those thoroughbreds are a little nervous for some cowboys, but for me, I love their speed and quickness."

The next morning I saddled Dean, a big, bay thoroughbred gelding. Because he was so tall I stood on a big rock to mount and then headed toward Maverick Pass. My legs were stiff from the previous day's long walk, but they soon loosened up as I jogged Dean along the mountain trail.

The roan was near where we had found him the day before, and I gave him a good running start down the ridge toward Independence

Valley. I was quite sure he would travel the same route we had taken before and try for the ridges after passing Holburn. It had worked for him once, why not again?

I crowded him only enough to keep him running, cutting every corner I could to save my saddle horse. When we were about two miles from Holburn the roan picked up speed and ran wild toward the spring. I supposed he sensed the time was near when he would again run away from me.

I stopped Dean and adjusted my saddle, pulling the cinches tight enough to hold the roan, for I was sure I would catch him this time. While the wild horse was running into Holburn and back out, I was casually trotting across country to intercept him. I hoped he might stop to drink, but it was not likely that he would because of the excitement.

I could see Peoho standing at the mud spring about a half mile away and wanted to ride over to check his condition, but the small trail of dust coming from Holburn told me the roan was getting near. I took my rope down and shook out a loop, then checked the honda knot I had tied a few days before. Dean and I were ready.

The roan closed the distance toward me, sure that he could run away when the time came. Dean was eager for the race and I had to hold him in tight rein to keep him from getting too far ahead of the wild horse. I didn't want the roan to cut out behind me again. We topped out on a wide, level, sage-covered bench nearly together. It was an excellent place for a race. I could see the roan strain for all the speed he could muster, and when he pulled ahead just a few yards I let Dean have his head. He ran erratically for a short distance before settling into those long, easy strides that ate up the distance rapidly and soon had me in roping position. I wanted this horse so much.

Realizing how easy it is to run a horse completely through the loop when throwing from behind the target, I cast my loop, and then yanked it tight when it had settled over the roan's head. I dallied three times around the horn and eased up on Dean, who didn't want to slow down. He still wanted to run—but the roan was captured.

I patted Dean and told him what a wonderful horse he was as we maneuvered the roan back to Squaw Creek. To say I was happy is an understatement. I was thrilled by our accomplishment.

Cheers greeted me when I led the roan into camp. I broke him to ride but he was always wild, and after two disturbing years he lay down and died. I know not for what reason—heartbreak perhaps.

I saw Peoho the next spring. He had a club foot and was unable to keep up with a bunch of horses, so he was all alone. When I called to him he gave me the whistle of a wild stallion. I was glad to see him so happy.

Bandana

Near evening snow started to fall, first in small, delicate flakes that melted as they hit the earth, darkening the ground with their moisture. By dark the storm had settled in, and large, fluffy clusters of snow filled the air, quietly settling to the earth and covering everything with an exquisite white mantle.

It was still snowing when Sid and I went out to grain our saddle horses in the early dark hours of the next morning. We were working for the Wine Cup cow outfit out of the H-D Ranch, part of a large spread owned by the Utah Construction Company. Art Sanders was the ranch foreman, and our job was to keep the cattle classed for feeding and to ride the adjacent range, keeping a close eye on the six hundred dry cows and steers on the Toana winter range.

Bordered on the north by the H-D Ranch and on the south by the Southern Pacific Railroad, Toana was really a long, flat draw about six miles wide and fifteen miles long. Long, low ridges came out from Thomas Mountain to the east and Black Mountain to the west. They were covered with scrub juniper, or cedar, and black sage, with bluebunch wheatgrass and Indian ricegrass the predominant forage. White sage and sweet sage were plentiful across the flat of the draw.

Two wells had been drilled so cattle could range out late in the fall and early winter, thus saving the considerable amount of hay they would normally eat. The six hundred head that were out would eat about six tons of hay each day on the feed ground.

Sitting at the breakfast table, we could hear the occasional low of cattle from below the corrals. They were probably cattle that had already trailed from the Toana, mostly old cows looking for a feed ground and a handout of hay.

"I see there is plenty of snow, Sid. Twenty-two inches out in the open from under the trees." Art tapped his yardstick against the door frame to shake the moisture from it.

"Come on and eat, Arthur," his wife Nellie said. "We don't have time to fool along with late comers. The eggs are getting cold."

"Be right there, honey. I had to measure the snow before it settles." Art was soon at the table.

"What about those cows on the Toana, Sid? Sounds like some of them have come home."

"We'll have to gather them as soon as we can, Art. Some of next year's calf crop will be in those dry cows. We don't want to lose any of them."

"Some steers out there too that need good feed for better growth," I chipped in.

"Ya, we don't want them to get poor." Sid paused momentarily, then having made a decision said, "As I see it, we need to ride today. There are only two of us so we could certainly use your help, Art."

"You've got it. What can I do?"

"We need a count on the cattle as they go into the field. There are probably at least a couple hundred along the fence now, and more coming. If you would count them into the warm spring field and have a man put a load of hay out at Three Mile, we can count again through the fence to the hay and be sure of what we have. Feed a quarter ton or a little less to the hundred for a day or two, and then increase gradually to full feed over about ten days. When we get them all we should have 617. I'll be surprised if everything comes in."

"Can the two of you ride that Toana country soon enough to save all the cattle?" Art asked.

"I'm sure we can. We'll ride the hills and cedars first. Push everything to the wells and trail in whenever we have a bunch. Most of them will follow our tracks to the ranch. The last few we'll have to ride for. Some of those old cows are good rustlers and may be way back in the hills. We can always track them if they're moving at all." After a pause Sid added, "I want to see which wild horses are in the area. If that big red sorrel Bandana is where we can get at him, I'd like to give him one more run."

"You've tried him several times haven't you, Sid?" Art asked.

"Five different times, and I've never been close to him. One time I caught Little Red, that horse Len Harrington rides, and another time I caught Alice Ann. Len rode him for awhile, too. Named the horse 'Alice Ann' after a red-headed girlfriend of his in Elko. He claims their hair is the same color—if that's a reason."

"What about the mustache?" I asked. "Does his gal have a red mustache like Alice Ann?" Everyone chuckled over that one.

"Alice Ann has the heaviest mustache of any horse I've ever seen. Icicles form on it and make him very touchy. Have either of you noticed how easy you have to be with the bit when you bridle him?" I talked on about Alice Ann, though I could tell Sid had more to say about the Bandana stud.

"Yes, I've noticed," Sid said. "I think it might be because some of the cowboys pull Alice Ann's mustache just for fun. They should know better. What I was saying about the red stud's bunch—I've taken a run at them five times and caught the two studs. Little Red comes from the big red stud for sure, but I think Alice Ann was sired by a different stallion. Maybe an older horse that had the bunch before Bandana. I judge the Bandana horse to be eight years old, possibly nine, and I want him before he's too old to be a useful saddle horse."

"You better catch him this winter then," Arthur cut in. "He'll be hard to handle if he's nine. Might not be worth the bother."

"Bother?" Sid quipped. "He won't be any bother."

Sid's eyes lighted up with excitement when he talked of wild horses. He would rather run at them than eat, almost. I watched with interest as the two bantered back and forth. With wild mustangs on their minds, there was no time to consider the cows and how to get them to the feed ground, only the wild horses and how the deep snow might affect their feed and travel conditions.

Finally, pushing back from the breakfast table, Art said, "Well, as I see it you'll have to find the red stud first. See what condition he's in and then decide what to do."

"You're right," Sid interjected. "That's just what I aim to do, and while I'm rounding up those cows on Toana, I'll find the stud. Want to wager on that, Art?"

"Not me. I know better than to bet against odds like that."

It took until December 10 to bring the cattle in from the Toana range. There were days of riding in snow up to our stirrups. First it would snow a few inches, settle a few, then snow again. They were hard, cold, wet days for both horse and rider. We tromped trail after trail to small bunches of cattle nestled in sheltered coves, cattle that otherwise would have stayed in seclusion and starved to death.

"Two days in Dead Man and we'll have it all covered," Sid said as we were eating our supper. "Two days left and I haven't seen anything of the Bandana stud. I saw two other bunches today. That makes seven bunches in all. About fifty head if I counted right. They'll have a rough go of it this winter, whether the snow keeps coming or not."

"Where would you guess Bandana is, Sid? Do you suppose he stayed over on Bishop Flat, maybe along by Cricket Springs? There's lots of tall sage there that will show above the snow."

"Could be that he's over there, but I think he might have stayed in the Brush Creek area. I'd try there first if I had time to look."

"Well, we'll have the cows in on feed in a few days. Maybe we could ride Brush Creek and see what's in there. Might be a few cows hid away in the brush or some of our work horses that should be put in the fifty-four field on the ryegrass."

"Let's figure on that," Sid said, "as soon as our horses rest a few days. They're a little leg-weary from this deep snow right now. We'll give them about a week."

We finished gathering the cattle and were pleased to count 632 head into the field. This was a few more than we turned out, so we figured some had been ranging around Thurston Spring or Dead Man Spring. However, we were sure we had found all of them.

Just after Christmas, Sid announced we would ride the Brush Creek area in search of cattle and maybe look at some work mares that ranged there. I felt Sid's decision coming on and had saved my best horse for the ride.

It was overcast, and not too cold the morning we rode into Brush Creek. The snow was still dragging our stirrups occasionally but was not crusted. We went past the main spring and saw no tracks at all. If there were animals nearby they were licking snow for moisture.

We climbed a bare swale to the top of the main ridge to observe the area below, looking into the dense brush and many swales where livestock might congregate.

There were about thirty deer among the cedars immediately north of the main spring, but there was no other sign of tracks in the snow until we came to the extreme north end of the ridge, where there was an assortment of tracks in the deep snow. Some were made by the deer we saw in the patch of cedars, but there were heavier tracks made by large animals, and a trail to the south.

"They're horse tracks," Sid said. "Cows don't move around like that in the deep snow."

Sid was excited and I figured he might be thinking of the big red stallion, Bandana.

"Let's cut the tracks near the point of the far ridge where they come together for the trail," Sid suggested as he turned Frosty toward the spot indicated.

I was riding Piute, my strongest and maybe my fastest saddle horse, a brown bally with white legs. His great long legs had kept my feet up out of the snow most of the day. Only in the short swales and drifts was the snow deep enough to reach my stirrups.

"It's horses," Sid said as we came to the trail. He turned along it, riding on a strong walk to an open area among the brush. "We better fix our saddles here before we come onto the bunch. I'm sure it must be the stud. Pull your cinch up pretty good. You might have to rope one." The excitement built as we prepared for the wild mustangs.

Nearly two hundred yards from where we adjusted our saddles, we topped a rise and rode into the middle of a large bunch of horses. I saw some of our work mares and a brown saddle horse we called Wolf. As I was looking for other familiar animals I heard Sid shout, "There he goes!" I turned toward the call and saw Sid urging Frosty in pursuit of the Bandana stallion. He was a big horse and though gaunt from lack of food, his long winter coat more than made up the difference in weight. He looked enormous as he plowed through the soft, deep snow toward Bishop Flat.

Nine other mustangs converged onto the trail behind Sid and were soon out of my sight. Quickly I glanced at the horses left behind. There were about twenty and they all acted gentle—at least they were not mustangs.

I followed at a good gallop, staying in the deep trail the eleven horses had made ahead of me. When I emerged from the heavy brush and came out on the lower slope of the ridge, I could see the race below me on the flat. Sid somehow had let the mustangs past him and was following the trail about a hundred yards to the rear. They were all trotting, and I was certain Piute could soon catch up. Another mile and Piute's long-stride trot and gallop brought me up to Sid.

"How's your horse?" Sid called.

"Good!" I shouted back.

"Give them a circle and bring them back to me. Don't let them beat you to the high brush in Willow Creek or they're gone!" Sid's words faded as I rode away.

I let my horse travel at his own pace, for he seemed eager to catch the mustangs. Less than half a mile of the trot and gallop and I was pushing close to the slowest horse. She was a mare, heavy with foal, and soon stopped just off the trail. Others, seeing what happened, turned to the side also, until the stallion was the only one ahead of us. We followed close behind him for another mile.

I was surprised at the ease with which Piute handled the deep snow, never faltering, never hesitating. I wondered if I should rope the stud but decided against it when I saw him flick his tail a few times. He was just about done. His strength was fully spent; the flick of his tail indicated to me he was about to give up.

I didn't want to kill his spirit, so I reined Piute out of the trail when I came to a place free of brush and urged him to outrun the stud. It didn't take much extra effort.

The stud stopped and stood somewhat spraddle-legged to brace himself. He wasn't as big as he had looked to be from a distance, maybe eleven hundred at the most.

I rode a few steps toward him and stopped. To crowd him now might cause him to fight or just give up and lie down, and I wanted him to retrace his trail so I could pick up the horses we had left behind.

The next time I moved he turned from me and started walking back along the trail. Each horse we came to nickered and reluctantly fell in line, following us back toward the gentle horses.

"He gave up on you, did he?" Sid asked. Then he looked at Piute and said, "That big brown horse is awesome in deep snow. He goes through it like it wasn't there. Not tired much either, is he?"

"Not tired at all. He's still pulling on the bit and looking for another race."

"Do you think we can put the mustangs back with the gentle horses and take all of them in together?"

"I don't know why not," I said. "More horses will make a better trail."

We picked up the gentle horses and trailed them all down to the fifty-four field. When we put them through the gate the stud refused to enter, so Sid ran him out through the brush and snow a short distance and roped him.

He was coming eight years old in the spring, a year younger than they had guessed he would be. There were also three young studs in the bunch—a yearling, and two that were two years old.

Bandana broke out gentle to ride but was always scared of a man on horseback. The younger studs were easily domesticated and grew up to become fine saddle horses.

The Rawhide Rope

Obtain the hide of a fat, two-year-old beef animal. The Jersey hide is too thin for me and the Holstein hide is thick, and thin under the spots—thicker under the dark spots.

Partially dry or freeze the hide to a consistency that is easy to cut with a sharp knife. Carve an oblong, circular chunk out of each side, rejecting the neck, back, flank, thin area of the belly, and any brands or scars.

You should now have two pieces of rawhide that are consistent in thickness. Use a good, sharp knife and strip each of these pieces into a long string about one inch wide by cutting around the chunk of hide until it is depleted.

Soak these rawhide strings in water and stretch them out along a fence or other area where they can dry or freeze. Scrape the hair from the string with a knife blade or other sharp object, taking care not to scar the hide.

Soak the strings again and dry to a damp condition. Pull them through a gauging instrument to cut the flesh side off and make the string a constant thickness. A sharp knife in a grooved board will do a good job if you are careful.

Now that you have stretched the string, taken the hair from it, and gauged off the flesh side, it is time to even the sides of the string and cut it to the width you wish to braid.

Cut a board so it has a straight shoulder on one side and a neck out from the shoulder over which to draw the string. Cut the wood of the neck the proper distance from the shoulder to effect a notch that will even one side of your string, probably near one-half inch.

Reverse the ends of the string and pull it through the gauge again, cutting to near one-quarter inch, or the width to make the string the size you wish to braid. Braid the string with the hair side out for better wear.

A six-strand rope would use a string about one-quarter inch wide. For a four-strand rope, about five-sixteenths. An eight-strand rein needs about a three-eighths-inch string—or any width you desire for the size item you wish to make. You can also braid around a small rope or wire, called putting a belly in it.

I braid an eight-strand rein square—with a belly it becomes round; six-strand can be round or hex—flat on the bottom and round on top; four-strand can be round or plaited—flat; and three-strand is flat.

Single strings are used to braid knots.

Beef tallow or fat is a better softener and preservative for rawhide. Some cowboys used liver on their ropes to make them soft and shiny, but I didn't care for it.

Most old-time dally men used fifty to sixty feet of rawhide rope, depending on the size of their hands.

The Rope Corral

We used a rope corral to confine our saddle horses so we could catch them for the day's work. The corral was made of one-inch seagrass rope, 150 feet long, strung in the shape of a round horseshoe with a loose rope across the opening where the horses entered. It was propped about thirty inches off the ground with forked sticks at about fifteen-foot intervals and held upright by two half-inch diameter guy ropes at each stick. Each end of the rope corral was braced with a double guy to make it more secure.

Figure about two feet of rope corral to the horse and allow for several to mill around in the center, and you can handle eighty head of saddle horses quite handily. If you have more horses in your cavy, you can split the bunch and bring in part at a time.

With our rope corral set up with the half-inch brace guys staked solidly, we were ready for the horses. A cavy of all gentle horses will walk right in and give no problem, but let's suppose we have eighty head, several of them broncs and three or four wild and unruly mustangs that show no trust in anyone.

First we effect a wing-out from each side of the fifty-foot opening to the corral by a cowboy taking the closing rope on a slight outward angle from one side; the other side of the wing is built with a lariat fastened to the corral and held by another cowboy. This forms a funnel to guide the horses into the corral and can be extended if necessary.

The horses enter the corral with the wild ones spooking and snorting, staying in the center of the gentle horses for protection. The long, closing rope is brought across behind them and a cowboy holds to it so he can let the mounts past one at a time as they are snaked out. Cowboys who are free, those not busy with something else, station themselves around the outer perimeter of the corral to help hold the horses in and to spot the ones wanted for the ride that day. Older horses walk to approximately the same place along the rope each time they are corralled and stand with their heads out over the rope, which hits them at about the top of the leg. They crowd close together and won't allow the young broncs up between them, controlling their area by biting or kicking. This leaves the wild horses to mill about in the center of an almost impregnable line of rumps.

The horses were herded out day and night so they could feed on fresh grass; they were cared for by a "nighthawk," a special rider hired for that purpose. Sometimes other regular cowboys assisted the nighthawk so he would have time needed to eat, sleep, or repair his riggin', a riggin' being his bridle, saddle, and chaps. Often it took one or two extra cowboys to bring the cavy in at daylight because about half the horses were mustangs in varying degrees of domesticity. In other words they were not all gentle.

With this many horses and several wild ones, it is certain there would be the nighthawk and another cowboy on horseback, and they would stay mounted with rope in hand to aid in any circumstance when needed. As each cowboy called the name of the horse he wanted, the boss or someone designated by him would lasso the horse and lead him out to be saddled. He either tossed the rope underhanded to catch the horse or flipped it overhanded; he had to be exceptionally accurate in order to catch only one horse at a time. It is best not to swing the loop, as this scares the broncs and more nervous horses in the center of the corral.

To demonstrate how solid the wall of horses was around the outer perimeter of the rope corral, I will tell you a true story.

It was summer, and we were branding calves for the Wine Cup cow outfit camped a few miles from the Eccles Ranch in Burnt Creek Canyon. There were seven of us at the time, not including the cook and wrangler. Three other cowboys had been sent to other areas to pick up some loose ends and would be back in a few days.

The cavy consisted of our two teams of four, about twenty horses belonging to the absent cowboys and an average of ten each for the seven of us plus six for the nighthawk. The rest of our cavy was in the high pasture above Loomis. It was a beautiful night, with a clear sky and the bright stars hanging just out of reach over our heads. The numerous stud piles reminded us we were in wild horse country, which kept us all alert hoping for a chance to catch one of them. We were also reminded that several of our saddle horses were wild and might leave with a bunch of wild horses should they mix with the cavy.

Ed was our nighthawk, and though he was not a throw 'em down, tie 'em up cowboy because one leg was much shorter than the other, he had a considerable amount of savvy about wild horses. He and Arnold were nighthawking the cavy when they heard a noise made by a trotting horse. Odd rustlings are easily detected in the still of the night.

"Ya got some horses leavin', Arnold! I can hear 'em trottin' away!" Ed called.

"Not me, Ed. It's quiet over here. The noise is between us. I think it's something trying to come in!"

At that moment a lone horse galloped into the bunch of saddle horses. The new horse spooked and snorted from horse to horse— very uneasy and nervous.

"A horse came in the herd close to me, Ed. It acts like a wild mustang. Let's back up and give it air. Maybe it will calm down enough to go in with the cavy." Arnold spoke quietly as Ed was riding up to him.

"I'll bet that's the mustang I saw alone out on the ridge yesterday," Ed offered. "I wondered if he would come in to see us."

"With him being alone he probably is a young stud. He's quieting a little. Might stay if we're careful. What time do you think it is, Ed?"

"When I struck that match awhile ago it was 3:15. We could start in any time now. I think we need help, though, if we expect to corral the mustang."

"Right," exclaimed Arnold. "You stay right here and I'll get some help. Be back in a few minutes." Arnold rode off into the night.

Johny and Sid, both good mustangers, went out with Arnold and maneuvered the wild mustang into the rope corral with the saddle horses. As soon as the older horses had taken their regular places around the rope corral, Sid rode quietly into the bunch and roped the young stud.

The horse was dark brown and had a small star in his forehead and one white hind foot. He was four years old and carried a few scars from battles he had engaged in while trying to win a harem. His conformation was good and he developed into a very useful saddle horse.

How to Catch a Wild Mustang

The preceding chapters describe a few of the encounters and some of the varied opportunities that come while chasing wild horses, and how my friends and I capitalized on them.

I look at my fine horsehide gloves and wonder if they weren't made from the hide of one of those wild mustangs or someone's pet saddle horse. It should be a reminder that hardly anything is entirely indispensable. We have to harvest one item in order to have the other. The best we can do when we harvest the mature is to replace it with the younger of the same species, thus insuring a continued harvest.

Just as there is more than one way to skin a cat, there is more than one way to catch a mustang. All ways are right ways; it is the end result that is important. A mustanger must be fully aware of each opportunity as it comes and act almost instantly to take complete advantage of it. Anything less will put him in a defensive situation, if not cause a complete loss. Generally there is no second chance.

Going after a wild horse after it has filled up on water is my first choice of ways to succeed. A mustang often goes from three to five days without water, depending on the amount of rain and succulence of the forage. When the horse comes in to drink after such a long time, it gorges itself with water, often waits a short time and then drinks again, sometimes staying close to water most of the day.

Just imagine how you would place in a race after drinking a bellyfull of water. You would come in last, and so does the mustang. After running about one-quarter mile, the wild animal's stomach cramps and he can run no more. This makes him an easy target for your loop.

Be careful with him after you have him roped. He will still not be feeling well and will need several minutes to recuperate.

My second choice is to follow the mustang in deep winter snows. If the snow is to your stirrups on a tall horse, you can trot the wild horse into submission. He makes the trail and you follow. The mustang is usually weak from eating rough, scarce food, while you have a strong, grain-fed horse. After a few miles the mustang can be roped easily. Sometimes you can hobble the first wild horse and continue after the bunch, and with a little luck you can catch a second horse. It depends entirely on the terrain and on the strength of your saddle horse.

Third in my judgment is a surprise attack. I get a thrill beyond comparison when I run at a bunch of mustangs and try to cut between the stallion and his harem. About seventy-five percent of the time, you can get close enough to the stud to catch him, or if he eludes your rope you still have a chance at another one of the bunch. Sometimes a wild stallion can strike fear into you as he charges with the thought of driving away an enemy, a challenging stud for instance. When he determines that a person is on the horse he quickly changes his plans, and this is when he is most vulnerable. I know of only one wild stud that ever charged a man with a rope, and that was only at the beginning of their encounter.

The relay is my fourth choice, ranked in this position because I hesitate to run a good saddle horse more than necessary. It could take all day to run a mustang down enough to catch it. I have known them to run about seventy miles and still be able to trot along. The low hills and desert are best for this, where you can keep in view of your quarry.

Next I would rank the trap corral. It must be built strong, but not completely solid; a wild mustang will enter a corral it can see through much more readily than one laced solid with brush and branches. It is better if you can run your horses downhill into the corral. Horses move easier downgrade when tired. This is also true of other animals, especially a deer when wounded.

Water trapping and other situations I bundle together. There is really no definite preference. It takes a unique situation to effect a good water trap, and I don't like the hard labor of building fences and gates, so I would rather take any of the other easier routes.

Some prefer to run mustangs in early spring, a good time because they are weak from the rough winter feed and the mares are heavy with foal. This very fact causes me to shy away from the early spring. I hesitate to take full advantage of the female process, regardless of which species it might be.

Whatever situation you choose, be assured that circumstances can arise that immediately alter your plans, and it is then necessary to take advantage of any opportunity afforded. Often when running to a corral you wind up with a wild horse on your rope, so keep it handy at all times.

Wild horses are now protected by the government. Maybe they should be declared game animals, giving the public a chance to buy permits and capture them under certain restrictions. Just a thought. There isn't enough feed for them to multiply without some restraint.